LITERARY INDUSTRIES

Chasing a Vanishing West

HUBERT HOWE BANCROFT

An Abridged Edition *by Kim Bancroft*

Foreword *by Kevin Starr*

Afterword *by Charles B. Faulhaber*

HEYDAY • BERKELEY, CALIFORNIA

This book was made possible in part by generous support from
Paul Bancroft III and The Friends of The Bancroft Library.

This is an abridgement of Hubert Howe Bancroft's *Literary Industries*,
first published in 1890 as volume 39 of *The Works of Hubert Howe Bancroft*
(The History Company: San Francisco, CA).

Library of Congress Cataloging-in-Publication Data
Bancroft, Hubert Howe, 1832-1918.
Literary industries : chasing a vanishing West / Hubert Howe
Bancroft ; an abridged edition by Kim Bancroft ; foreword by
KevinStarr ; afterword by Charles B. Faulhaber.
pages cm
"This is an abridgement of Hubert Howe Bancroft's Literary
Idustries, first published in 1890 as volume 39 of The Works of
Hubert Howe Bancroft (The History Company: San Francisco, CA.)"—
Title page verso.
With a new subtitle and edited to focus on Bancroft's autobiography.
Includes bibliographical references and index.
ISBN 978-1-59714-248-9 (pbk. : alk. paper)
1. Bancroft, Hubert Howe, 1832-1918. 2. Historians—United States—Biography.
3. Booksellers and bookselling—United States—Biography. 4. Book industries
and trade—United States. I. Bancroft, Kim, editor. II. Title.
E175.5.B22A3 2014
978.007202—dc23
[B]   2013028686

Cover Design: Leigh McLellan Design
Cover Art and Frontispiece: Hubert Howe Bancroft, courtesy of
The Bancroft Library; Bancroft, Hubert Howe—POR 14
Editor Photo: Kate Black
Interior Design/Typesetting: Leigh McLellan Design
Printed in Canada by Friesens

Orders, inquiries, and correspondence should be addressed to:
Heyday
P.O. Box 9145, Berkeley, CA 94709
(510) 549-3564, Fax (510) 549-1889
www.heydaybooks.com

10 9 8 7 6 5 4 3 2 1

CONTENTS

ILLUSTRATIONS

FOREWORD

Kevin Starr

AUTOBIOGRAPHY OFFERS AN opportunity for self-discovery, self-invention, and self-justification. In *Literary Industries* (1890), Hubert Howe Bancroft (1832–1918)—bookseller, library collector, man of letters, archdruid of nineteenth-century historiography—pursues each of these purposes to great effect, while at the same time keeping them in balance. If any one of these functions dominates, an autobiography can suffer; but when definition, justification, and dream wish are admixed in just the right proportions—as they are in, say, Benjamin Franklin's *Autobiography* (the complete version first published in 1868), Mark Twain's *Roughing It* (1872), and *The Education of Henry Adams* (1907)—the result is literature, in all its aspiration and ambiguity, as well as historical record, in all its regard for fact. Because Bancroft gives this dynamic interaction of conscious and subconscious purpose anchored in personal story, *Literary Industries* remains relevant to autobiography as a genre as well as to the rise of American historiography in the late nineteenth century, and to the search by California apologists of that era for significance and authentication. *Literary Industries* also remains relevant to the various professions Bancroft embraced with such success—bookselling, library development, historiography—in the course of his long life.

As a literary form, autobiography is also enmeshed in, contingent with, and presented through social setting and event: the wider world, in brief, that has influenced, energized, or thwarted the autobiographer and in turn been shaped and expressed, for better or for worse, by the autobiographer telling the story. From this perspective, Bancroft opens his narrative and sustains it throughout with an evocation of—and wrestling with—the New England tradition, as translated by his Yankee forebearers from New England to Ohio. For Bancroft, who frequently describes himself as a Puritan or quasi-Puritan, his New England ancestry—Anglo-American in descent, Presbyterian in religion, literary and historical in intellectual formation—demands of him from the beginning that he find something significant to do with his life—something touched by greatness—and then get on with the task. No Puritan divine, no Cotton Mather in his Boston study writing the *Magnalia Christi Americana* (1702), offers more vignettes of devotion to duty, to the demanding intellectual, physical, financial, emotional, as well as intellectual task of making available to the Pacific states of Central and North America—one-twelfth of the world's population, as Bancroft points out—the history they at once deserve and require if they are to fulfill their collective destiny.

New England and its Puritan heritage are evident as well in Bancroft's repeated remarks about the horrors of wasting time, the distractions of social life, and the dissipations—especially in youth—of card playing, with its whiff of the diabolical and the occult, as well as the vices of alcohol and tobacco (up to a full bottle of claret or sherry per day in his youth, he admits, as well as four or five cigars!), and dancing. Yes, dancing! Dancing all night on a number of occasions. This repeated abjuration of dancing suggests to the reader that the historian and bookseller of late middle age is recalling something a little more intimate than mere dancing in the long lost days of his youth when he now and then went astray before his first wife and the Calvary

Presbyterian Church in San Francisco threw out the lifeline and pulled the young sinner safely to shore.

New England as well is not only to credit for Bancroft's discovery of his calling but was to have the first fruits of that labor: the bound galleys of the first volume of *Native Races* (5 vols., 1874–1875), read and publicly endorsed by the literary worthies of Boston and Cambridge. Not having attended Harvard or Yale or some comparable institution, and remaining somewhat sensitive about it, Bancroft wanted acceptance by those communities and, traveling east with a suitcase of bound galleys, he secured an extraordinary array of endorsements from such figures as poet and essayist James Russell Lowell, poet John Greenleaf Whittier, essayist and poet Ralph Waldo Emerson, historian Francis Parkman, editor of *The Atlantic Monthly* William Dean Howells, and historian and secretary of the Navy George Bancroft (no relation, H. H. tells us, although later genealogical research says otherwise).

Yet the effort to win such notice and approval left him emotionally exhausted, to the point that he took to his bed for a fortnight to recover. Seeking such approval spoke to Bancroft's reverence for the New England tradition, true. But it also worked directly against his sense of being a self-made man in a self-made state, pioneering a self-made way of researching and writing history decades before, Bancroft goes out of his way to tell us, Harvard librarian Justin Winsor produced a comparable effort in his *Narrative and Critical History of America* (8 vols., 1884–1889), to which Winsor contributed his own work as well as including the work of others.

In Melville's *Moby-Dick* (1851), Ishmael tells the reader that a whaling ship was his Harvard and Yale: the place where he came to maturity, insight, strength, and resolve. For Bancroft, as he reveals himself in *Literary Industries*, the California gold rush was his undergraduate college, and the rising city of San

Francisco his post-graduate course in business and book collecting, and in the writing of history. Bancroft was proud of his youthful strength, as well as his love of the outdoors, but after nearly a year of hard physical work in the mines, he drew upon his earlier experience in upstate New York and entered the book trade, first as a wholesale importer and jobber of books, receiving shipments from the East Coast for retail sale in West Coast mining settlements. Resettled in San Francisco in the mid-1850s, he advanced to the next stage of business development as part of the larger momentum of this rapidly growing maritime colony on the Pacific, then in the throes of what Bancroft would later describe as a "rapid, monstrous maturity." With money already earned, he assembled several fifty-vara lots between Market and Stevenson Streets, fronting on Market, and in rapid order had designed and constructed there an impressive headquarters for his multiple enterprises: printing presses in the basement, their weight borne by the ground; books, stationery, and related sundries for retail sale on the ground and second floors; and, as it soon turned out, library space on the second and third floors for his growing collection (60,000 volumes, a half-mile of library shelving, he proudly tell us); and on the top floor his own office (as well as a pied-à-terre for late-night work), with work stations for a growing corps of researchers as well as two residential rooms for favored employees.

Bookselling led to book collection for purposes of researching publications, and this in turn led to the creation of one of the two great libraries of San Francisco, the other being that assembled by mining engineer Adolph Sutro at a slightly later period. Had Hubert Howe Bancroft been merely a bookseller, it would have sufficed. Had he only gained a reputation as a businessman, bookseller, and library developer, it would have earned him mention in the annals. But Bancroft wanted more, and this hunger for more, for something epic in intent and achievement, grew naturally out of what he was already doing, and alongside a certain zeitgeist in San Francisco he suggests through his brief discussion of the pioneering San Francisco historian Franklin Tuthill, author of *The History of California* (1866). The American frontier in California did not represent an escape from history, or even a disjunctive new beginning. It was, rather, a fulfillment of long development, a guide for corrective action in the present, and a pathway to the future.

As astonishing as Bancroft's multivolume *History of the Pacific States of North America* (1874–1890) might seem in retrospect—a Mount Shasta of scholarship rising from a level plain, a trans-Sierran track of hefty volumes connecting the frontier to the East—history, Bancroft suggests, was part of the American frontier from the beginning. Robert Greenhow, a librarian and archivist with the Department of State in Washington, DC, researched and wrote *The History of Oregon and California* (1844) as part of the very process that created the mentality of Manifest Destiny that led to the seizure of California by the United States in 1846. Publisher John Frost produced a *Pictorial History of California* (1850) from his history-writing factory in Philadelphia that anticipated Bancroft's later methods. New York attorney Elisha Smith Capron spent a few months in California in 1853 as the agent for several New York firms, then returned East to produce yet another *History of California* (1854). In *Literary Industries*, Bancroft dates the beginning of his San Francisco life to 1856, one year after the appearance of *The Annals of San Francisco* (1855), an 800-plus-page behemoth written by journalists Frank Soulé, John H. Gihon, and James Nisbet, which Bancroft, now a bookseller, described as a book designed to sell. Isaac Cox produced *The Annals of Trinity County* (1858), the first of 150 county histories to be written between then and 1900. Most importantly, there was Franklin Tuthill's 1866 *History*, written in his evening hours by the editor of the San Francisco *Bulletin*, and praised by

Bancroft as "the first *History of California* deserving the title" for Tuthill's use of European archives, which he visited while traveling for his health.

The writing of history was in the air in San Francisco, but Bancroft soon began to take it to an entirely new level in terms of resources and scope. Like Greenhow and Tuthill, Bancroft understood the importance of European archives in tracing the early exploration and settlement of the Pacific Coast. Accordingly, he visited London and Paris and, with his usual prodigality and omnivorousness, collected or copied, or had copied by others, an extraordinary array of primary and/or archival sources. Two decades and more before the rise of historical ethnography, Bancroft anchored his series in a five-volume consideration of aboriginal life, *Native Races*, which remains valuable as a resource to this day. A half century before the commencement of the Herbert Eugene Bolton era at The Bancroft Library at the University of California, Berkeley—the very library Bancroft formed and institutionalized in a grand building on Valencia Street in San Francisco and eventually sold to the University of California—Bancroft discerned, researched, and presented the history of Central America, Mexico, and the Spanish borderlands in interaction with the United States, the British-dominated Oregon Territory (now Oregon and Washington) and British Columbia, and the Russian-founded, American-purchased Alaska.

In their considerations of the Hispanic experience, the Bancroft histories keep a certain distance from Roman Catholicism and its institutions. As Bancroft tells us in *Literary Industries*, Archbishop Joseph Sadoc Alemany of San Francisco wanted a right of review of the final product if he were to open to him the archives of the Archdiocese of San Francisco, but Bancroft refused the offer. On the other hand, Bancroft purchased or had copied in Mexico City and elsewhere whatever he could find pertaining to the mission as a frontier institution (Bolton's later term) and related Spanish subjects, and he was indefatigable in his collecting of manuscripts and interviewing for transcription the surviving Hispanic pioneers of Southern and Northern California. In this effort, he enlisted the assistance of General Mariano Vallejo and the lovable (if not always believable) Henry Cerruti, who collected manuscripts and interviews that would, along with printed materials, energize the flowering of the Bolton school of borderland historiography in the first half of the twentieth century. Like the Franciscan explorer Silvestre Escalante, Bancroft trekked eastward through Nevada, which he appropriated to his epic, and on to Utah, for which his series achieved an early and balanced consideration of the Mormon experience, having made connection with the apostles and historians of that beleaguered church.

Now comes the difficult part, the question Was Hubert Howe Bancroft being fully honest when he put his name, exclusively, as author on each and every one of the volumes of the *History of the Pacific States*? In *Literary Industries* (which was published as the final installment, volume 39, of the series), Bancroft goes out of his way to give credit to such figures as Henry Lebbeus Oak and Frances Fuller Victor and the others whom he employed to advance his history-making enterprise, including the unnamed scores of clerks and readers who helped prepare the topical index to his collection, which allowed it to be accessed and utilized in its totality. He wrote each volume, Bancroft claims, from arrangements of material and drafts presented to him by his researchers.

Given the sweep and scale of *History of the Pacific States*, it is difficult to assess Bancroft's claim, and we must remember, incidentally, that he does not overly press the point. Did he truly create each volume from these previously prepared building blocks? Henry Lebbeus Oak, a longtime employee frequently mentioned in *Literary Industries*, later openly claimed authorship for the seven-volume *History of California* that Bancroft signed as his own. Critics have also claimed comparable authorship for Frances Fuller Victor in the case of the Oregon volumes.

Hubert Howe Bancroft knew how to write—that is for sure. *California Pastoral* (1888), an evocation of the Hispanic era; *California Inter Pocula* (1888), an impressionistic portrayal of the gold rush; *Popular Tribunals* (1887), a study of the mining era with an emphasis upon the law-and-order question; *Essays and Miscellany* (1890); and *Literary Industries*—these have been judged to be almost exclusively his own. They are well-written books, lively and comprehensive. *Literary Industries*, the most personal and personally written of his books, is in a class of its own.

Given contemporary concern for intellectual property rights, the unease surrounding Bancroft's exclusive use of his own authorial byline is totally understandable. Would not Hubert Howe Bancroft, we ask ourselves, have survived as an equally impressive founder of the historiography of the Pacific states had he, as in the case of Lord John Acton in *The Cambridge Modern History*, merely listed himself as the editor of the series, signed the five volumes he wrote, and granted some form of credit to other writers who played substantial roles in the composition of other volumes? Certainly Lord Acton, Bancroft's contemporary, lost no lustre for choosing this solution; and certainly as well, the full greatness of Hubert Howe Bancroft's achievement has been, and perhaps remains, obscured by his overreaching.

Bancroft pioneered the industrial system of history writing. Without such a system, as he correctly argues, nothing like the *History of the Pacific States* would have been produced out of the San Francisco of the mid- to late nineteenth century. Unlike Lord Acton, Bancroft did not have the resources of a centuries-old university and its respected scholars to draw upon. The University of California was decades away from anything approaching such maturity. True, Bancroft's contemporary, Theodore Henry

Hittell (1830–1917), who goes unmentioned in *Literary Industries*, researched and wrote on his own a four-volume *History of California* (1885–1897). Hittell, however, a distinguished attorney, prodigious in his research, remained within the confines of California history from a legal perspective. Bancroft, by contrast, wanted it all: he wanted to produce the history of the entire Pacific region, and as the calculations he presents in *Literary Industries* show, there was no way he could do this outside the industrialized model he created.

Put aside for the moment the question of Bancroft's overreaching authorship; or, rather, put this question within the context of the total achievement of the *History of the Pacific States*. There is an old adage: you cannot have Falstaff and have him thin. The fundamental genius of Hubert Howe Bancroft lies in the fact that he envisioned such a comprehensive history, assembled its materials, set researchers and writers to work, and produced, published, and marketed History with a capital H—as in the History with a capital H he had emblazoned over the entrance of the History Building he built on Market Street when his longtime first building was destroyed by fire in 1886.

At a time when the Far West was evolving its systems and institutions in the public and private sector, Bancroft ensured that the creation of research libraries and the writing, publishing, and reading of history would be part of this agenda—as essential, in fact, as railroads, shipping, agriculture, construction, banking, and the founding of universities and colleges. From this perspective, Hubert Howe Bancroft achieved something of the greatness he had always hungered for but feared might elude him. A mid- and late Victorian, typical of his era, Bancroft understood and appreciated money and business, but he aspired as well, like his California contemporary Josiah Royce, to a connection to higher meaning. In Bancroft's case, that higher meaning was the march of Progress, in which he never lost faith. Hubert Howe

Bancroft loved his family, his business, his books, his histories. In the emergence of California and San Francisco in the mid- to late nineteenth century, he achieved the status of Founder in the library he had created. In the books he commissioned and published, the books he wrote himself, and above all in *Literary Industries*, we can hear his voice, experience his fears and losses, and take satisfaction in the record he has left us of a life well lived to productive purposes.

PREFACE

Kim Bancroft

"Books! books! I revelled in books....I would bathe
my mind in them till saturated with the better part of
their contents." —H. H. Bancroft, *Literary Industries*

I WAS NINE YEARS OLD in 1967 when James D. Hart, the
Director of The Bancroft Library at UC Berkeley, gave my
parents, my three brothers, and me a tour of the Bancroft stacks.
In those days, you could see down through the metal floors and
up through the metal ceilings to shelving that reached forever.
The antique books and specially fastened boxes contained California's history, Mr. Hart explained, "and *your* history," he added,
referring to my great-great-grandfather, Hubert Howe Bancroft,
always "H. H." to the family.

Mr. Hart came to a shelf of musty, thin, leather-backed books.
"Bancroft used these to collect stories of Mexican Californios
and American pioneers in the early West," he informed us. Then
moving to a set of books bound in tanned cowhide, Hart pulled
one down and opened to a page of graceful script in faint ink.
"These are diaries your great-great-grandmother Matilda kept
for each of her four children, among others she wrote about her
early marriage and family travels." Randomly picking a passage,
Hart read Matilda's description of Lucy, Matilda and Hubert's
only daughter, raging at her three older brothers, Paul, Griffing,

and Philip, as they left her behind to hunt for frogs in Walnut Creek (when it really was a creek and not a city).

Later at home, I approached the shelves of the thirty-nine thick volumes stamped with *Bancroft's Works* in gold on the spines. Where could I find those stories to learn about this family, the pioneers, and the Indians? I pulled down volume 39, called *Literary Industries*, the book that my father, Paul Bancroft III, had said was H. H.'s autobiography. I opened to the picture of the strangely mustached old man. Then I confronted his elaborate Victorian verbiage, 800 pages thick. Daunted, I put the book away—for over four decades.

I finally did return to the library of Hubert Howe Bancroft and his *Works*, now with an adult's curiosity, eager to understand who he was, how he lived, and how he had collected and written his history of the Pacific states. Of course, the best place to answer my queries was where I had left off: Bancroft's 1890 autobiography, *Literary Industries*.

When I again opened this tome, H. H.'s enthusiastic introduction to the Pacific Coast territories now drew me in, his awe and optimism vibrant as he reports his task: "to save to the world a mass of valuable human experiences, which otherwise, in the hurry and scramble attending the securing of wealth, power, or place in this new field of enterprise, would have dropped out of existence." Here was a man on a mission.

And what a mission that was, I learned, after reading all 800 pages. Ultimately, Bancroft collected 60,000 books and documents, wrote or oversaw the research and writing of 38 volumes of history, and created a library now comprising 6 million books and documents, materials essential to one of the most stellar research institutions in all the world.

How had H. H. been able to accomplish all that scholarship without even a college education? How had he kept his bookselling and publishing businesses viable while pursuing his literary enterprise? And all this while managing properties distant from his San Francisco base, overcoming terrible personal tragedies, and raising a brood of children.

Literary Industries answers those questions through H. H.'s honest and often delightfully wry self-analysis. He shares not only his journey toward a new life in California in 1852 but also his struggles to overcome his "extreme sensitiveness" and his insecurity about his qualifications as a scholar. On a practical level, Bancroft elucidates his expertise in running a successful business and relates the pleasures he takes from hard work, from writing, and from the state he came to love so deeply.

As I first read *Literary Industries*, Bancroft's instructive aphorisms and his humorous and apt commentary surprised me, so applicable they were to life even today. He describes the value of reading and learning: "A healthy cultivated mind never can be lonely; all the universe is its companion." Anyone who grew up as a bookworm—especially shy or lonely—can appreciate how Bancroft captures the companionship of books and the nobility of cultivating our minds through bookish escapes.

Also surprising was the relevance of H. H.'s social commentary. He disparages a society seemingly turned from relying on "necessary labor,…the honorable and praiseworthy enterprise incident to life and independence" in favor of "an avaricious pursuit of wealth for the sake of wealth." How aptly ring these words today, when conspicuous consumption expands as our homes do. Bancroft, too, questioned his own costly consumption of the books and documents that he was gathering for his library, like a crazed "bibliomaniac," but he defended his collecting as a lofty goal: to secure to all humanity "more full and complete early historical data than any government or people on earth enjoy to-day."

On a very personal level, I found Bancroft's elegies on nature inspiring, having recently moved to a simple cabin in the woods, far removed from urban life. H. H. rhapsodizes that "thought is liberated" in the countryside: "Often many a one with an exquisite sense of relief escapes from the din and clatter of the city, and the harassing anxieties of business, to the soft sensuous quiet of the country, with its hazy light, aromatic air, and sweet songs of birds." Indeed. As Bancroft notes, "Nothing can exceed the satisfaction, if indeed congenial and comfortable, of a room in a country cottage." Off the electrical grid in my own woodland cottage, I read this book long into many winter nights, relying on kerosene lamps when my solar panels failed me, but the cabin stayed snugly warm with the heat of a wood stove. I imagined myself living much as H. H. and Matilda did in the late 1870s and '80s, when Matilda would edit her husband's writing as they warmed themselves by the hearth in a parlor lit by oil lamps.

Enchanted by H. H.'s edifying philosophies, his perspective on early California history, and stories that shed light on my own family history, I copied out passages to share with my brothers and father. Then I tried to rally interest in a family book club to read *Literary Industries* together, with a modern spin: a blog for exchanging commentary. Soon my siblings and father dropped out, like most people who have attempted the tome, overwhelmed after a few chapters. I persevered alone.

At The Bancroft Library one day, I encountered Charles Faulhaber, then the Library Director, and reported that I was enjoying reading *Literary Industries*. He laughed, "I've always said that there's a good *short* book in there."

Well, yes! Thus began my self-imposed challenge to edit *Literary Industries* into "a good *short* book," one easily read to the very end.

Just as H. H. uses *Literary Industries* to document the causes that drove him to his literary pursuits, I explain here my editing of his work. I, too, wished to save to the world the valuable experiences that Bancroft conveyed in his autobiography and which have significance for several audiences.

As Kevin Starr describes in his Foreword, *Literary Industries* reflects California life in a remarkable time, from the perspective of a man who had the perspicacity and energy to collect history while it was transpiring in the tumultuous years following the gold rush. H. H. was committed to saving what records he could, even as that early Western history was vanishing. Arriving in California in 1852 hard upon the Forty-Niners, Bancroft could foresee a powerful destiny for the Pacific West and was determined to provide an encyclopedic record in *Bancroft's Works*, using the resources of his personal library. Bancroft's story, then, becomes representative of many of those who came to California to make a new life for themselves and for the United States.

While only serious historians of the West utilize *Bancroft's Works* today, The Bancroft Library is in great demand. As Charles Faulhaber describes in his Afterword, the library is surely Bancroft's best work. The 60,000 documents H. H. gathered reflect a unique vision of collecting, unusual at the time, for he not only sought scholarly works on the West, but he also saved newspapers and pamphlets, documents later called "junk" by some detractors but valued today by those exploring life at the grass roots of Bancroft's time. Subsequent Bancroft Library curators and directors have expanded on Bancroft's vision of preserving a range of texts and artifacts. Now scholars the world over arrive at the library to analyze human nature and society, from ancient Egypt to the latest cultural movements.

Those interested in Bancroft's scholarly contributions to the history of the West will be well informed by this abridged *Literary*

Industries, and those deeply interested are encouraged to return to the original volume to discover what has been left out here.

And what has been excised? Certain categories of Bancroft's original did not make the final cut. First and easiest to eliminate were the many verbose musings of a well-educated (albeit autodidactic) Victorian gentleman, such as his complaints about the unreliability of newspapers in his time, the unsuitability of women for difficult literary work, or the need for maintaining bodily health in relation to mental productivity. Exhibiting his erudition, Bancroft buttressed such disquisitions at length by multiple quotations from other writers. The abridged version captures his key arguments without the belabored exegesis for which modern readers have no patience. (Perhaps his readers of yore skipped around liberally as well, but they were surely less distracted by the competing information we face today from electronic devices of all kinds.)

A second category excised was Bancroft's extensive defense of his work. The man adored scholarship but never attended college. We sense the chip on his shoulder when he describes how the intelligentsia of his time would decry him as a mere "shopkeeper" who presumed he could write history. So Bancroft highlights the laudatory reviews his histories received, quoting at length to prove the value of his work. I retained some of these comments to demonstrate the support he received and deserved, without overwhelming the modern reader.

Bancroft also defends the necessity of utilizing the many research and writing assistants who helped him over a period of two decades. Were he to write all those volumes by himself, Bancroft explains, it would have taken four hundred years. However, he never concedes that he should have given them more credit in the volumes they wrote themselves.

This point is related to the third area that I cut substantially: Bancroft's description of the "men on the fifth floor." Bancroft took umbrage at the criticisms launched at him for failing to acknowledge fully the many fine assistants who helped complete *Bancroft's Works.* Seeking to allay those criticisms, he devoted thirty pages of *Literary Industries* to details about each of the men—and the one woman allowed to join his ranks—who had collected documents, researched information, and written the histories. Several of Bancroft's descriptions of his most notable assistants, here included, show the great esteem Bancroft held for the scholars in his library, many of international origins and well educated, having attended college, unlike their employer.

Also excised were extensive details regarding Bancroft's *modus operandi* in collecting and using his library to write his *Works.* Around 1860 he began to assemble information for a business directory of the Pacific Coast. As he continued to gather books on the West, far beyond those needed for his original plan, Bancroft struggled to find a purpose for his collection, aside from his passion for the subject matter of the developing Pacific Coast. The plan for his collection gradually evolved into the creation of an encyclopedia, but he later abandoned even that idea as too narrow. At last he embraced the vision of a history of the whole Pacific West, from Central America to Canada. As his collection grew, he and his assistants experimented with various methods to wrestle the unwieldy mass of material into useable form. We who rely on computers today for help with input, storage, organization, and other research-related labor can only gape at the way Bancroft and his assistants confronted these tasks, using paper bags and index cards newly invented specifically for the purpose. The essence of his methods has been preserved here, but those interested in the fine points of Bancroft's collection and distillation processes will want to delve into the original.

As for my own methods of patching together sentences and passages after excising text, I sought to remain true to Bancroft's phrasing, including his usage and punctuation. To bridge a gap between one passage and another, I inserted words already in his text or added as few new words as possible to form a transition.

I have also added endnotes that will shed light on some of the historical and literary figures and events Bancroft mentions. Even a short biographical note indicates the cultural contributions of the many talented people Bancroft personally knew and whose stories he tried to capture for his histories and library. The bibliography further provides a reference for those interested in finding some of the papers that Bancroft and his assistants collected, still lodged in The Bancroft Library.

Ironically, H. H. declared that he refused to allow anyone to change his words. He reports the Archbishop of San Francisco announcing that he was "taking it for granted that you will let me see before publication what is written on religious matters, lest unintentionally something might be stated inaccurately, which no doubt you would rectify." Bancroft wrote, "It is needless to say that neither to the archbishop, nor to any person, living or dead, did I ever grant permission to revise or change my writings."

Happily, H. H. limited his rejection of editors to the "living or dead." He could not anticipate that his future great-great-granddaughter would revise his writing.

As a historian, Bancroft aimed to lay enough facts before his readers so they might make their own judgments as to the truth. He told his own story in the same way, asking readers to understand him fully. Because extensive cutting was necessary, many of Bancroft's richly descriptive stories had to be left out. Imagine, then, how much of his full life he himself had already eliminated:

> I cannot mention in this volume a hundredth part of the journeys made, the people seen, and the work done in connection with the labors of over a quarter of a century, collecting material and writing history, but enough has

been presented to give the reader some faint conception of the time, labor, and money necessary for such an historical undertaking.

I hope that this rendering of *Literary Industries* will still provide a full and fulfilling impression of Bancroft's life and work.

What remains is a beautifully written narrative of a man who inspires by his example and provokes inquiry with his contradictions. Bancroft's sensitivity, his love of California, his hard work for the benefit of his beloved state, and his commitment to writing and scholarship all set a fine example, including for readers today.

As this version of H. H.'s autobiography returns to life, it is appropriate that his own Bancroft Library should oversee its publication in conjunction with the help of two fine intellectuals and businessmen. One is my father, Paul (Pete) Bancroft III, himself a successful entrepreneur in the very image of his great-grandfather. My father's deep interest in the world was an abiding topic in our childhood. In encouraging the rewriting and publication of *Literary Industries*, Paul would make H. H. very proud.

Finally, it is most fitting that *Literary Industries* is being reissued by Malcolm Margolin's press Heyday, one of California's finest publishers. Margolin, like H. H. Bancroft, was once a youth come to California and unsure of his future. Also like H. H., Malcolm began to write and then publish and sell books that celebrate California in its rich diversity, from the very ecology of the land itself to the many cultures to whom Heyday's publications have now given a voice. Bancroft's romance with the magic of making books resonates with Heyday's gift to California. Book making, said Bancroft, entails the "metamorphoses of mind into manuscript, and manuscript into permanent print; the incarnation of ideas, spreading your thoughts first upon paper and then transfixing them by the aid of metal to the printed page, where through the ages they may remain, display a magic."

In addition to my gratitude to Malcolm at Heyday, I would like to acknowledge the invaluable guidance and patience from all the staff at Heyday, including the help of editor Gayle Wattawa and production manager Diane Lee, in gracefully shepherding the book through the various book-making steps, as well as Leigh McLellan's gorgeous design work.

I'd especially like to thank Susan Snyder, the head of Public Services at The Bancroft Library, for finding so many wonderful illustrations from the library's collection. I also want to acknowledge Elaine Tennant, director of The Bancroft Library, for her wisdom in helping to create a beautiful keepsake for all time in honor of H. H. Bancroft and his library. The support of the Council of Friends of The Bancroft Library also helped make *Literary Industries* return to life. And finally, thanks to Charles Faulhaber, former director of The Bancroft, for instigating this edition with his brilliant idea of finding "a good short book" in the original tome.

And so H. H. Bancroft's life—achievements and foibles all— endures into a new age.

LITERARY INDUSTRIES

I

THE FIELD

I T IS NOW OVER thirty years since I entered upon the task to-day accomplished. During this period my efforts have been continuous. Sickness and death have made felt their presence; financial storms have swept over the land, leaving ghastly scars; calamities more or less severe have at various times called at my door; yet have I never been wholly overwhelmed, or reached a point where was forced upon me a cessation of library labors, even for a single day. Nor has my work been irksome; never have I lost interest or enthusiasm; never have I regretted the consecration of my life to this cause, or felt that my abilities might have been better employed in some one of the great enterprises attending the material development of this western world, or in accumulating property, which was never a difficult thing for me to do. It has been from first to last a labor of love, its importance ever standing before me paramount to that of any other undertaking in which I could engage, while of this world's goods I have felt that I had always my share, and have been ready to thank God for the means necessary to carry forward my work to its full completion. And while keenly alive to my lack of ability to perform the task as it ought to be done, I have all the time been conscious that it were a thousand times better it should be done as I could do it than not at all.

What was this task? It was first of all to save to the world a mass of valuable human experiences, which otherwise, in the hurry and scramble attending the securing of wealth, power, or place in this new field of enterprise, would have dropped out of existence. These experiences were all the more valuable for the fact that they were new; the conditions attending their origin and evolution never had before existed in the history of mankind, and never could occur again. There was here on this coast the ringing-up of universal intelligence for the final display of what man can do at his best, with all the powers of the past united, and surrounded by conditions such as had never before fallen to the lot of man to enjoy.

Secondly, having secured to the race a vast amount of valuable knowledge which otherwise would have passed into oblivion, my next task was to extract from this mass what would most interest people in history and biography, to properly classify and arrange the same, and then to write it out and so place within reach all this gathered knowledge, in the form of a history. Meanwhile the work of collecting books and documents on Pacific coast history continued, while I erected a refuge of safety for the final preservation of the library, in the form of a fire-proof brick building on Valencia street, in the city of San Francisco.

Had this plan so presented itself, and with no alternative, I never should have had the courage to undertake it. It was because I was led on by my fate, following blindly in paths where there was no returning, that I finally became so lost in my labors that my only way out was to finish them. I cannot but feel that I was but the humble instrument of some power mightier than I, call it providence, fate, environment, or what you will. That I should leave my home and friends at the east and come to this coast an unsophisticated boy, having in hand and mind the great purpose of securing to a series of commonwealths, destined to be second in intelligence and importance to none the sun has ever shone upon, more full and complete early historical data than any government or people on earth enjoy to-day, is not for a moment to be regarded as the facts of the case. It was the vital expression of a compelling energy.

Presenting here a history of my history, an explanation of my life, its efforts and accomplishments, there should be established in the mind of the reader a good and sufficient reason for the same. In any of the departments of human activity, he alone can reasonably ask to be heard who has some new application of ideas; something to say which has never been said before; or, if said before, then something which can be better said this second or twentieth time. I do not only deal in new facts, but in little else; in facts brought out in this latter-day dispensation as a revelation of development as marvelous in its origin and as magical in its results as any appearing upon the breaking up of the great dark age preceding the world's uncovering and enlightenment. The faithful recorder of the events must be at once poet and prophet of the new dispensation.

The proposition stands thus: As the author's life has been mainly devoted to this labor, and not his alone but that of many others, and as the work has been extensive and altogether different from any which has hitherto been accomplished in any other part of the globe, it was thought that it might prove of interest if he should present a report, setting forth what he has accomplished and how he accomplished it. Coming to this coast a boy, he has seen it transformed from a wilderness into a garden of latter-day civilization, vast areas between the mountains and the sea which were at first pronounced valueless unfolding into homes of refinement and progress. There is now being planted a civilization destined in time to be superior to any now existing; and as to coming millions, if not to those now here, everything connected with the efforts of the builders of the commonwealths on these shores will be of vital interest—it seems not out of place to devote the last volume of his historical series to an account of his labors in this field.

IN THE UNFOLDINGS of my fate, I found myself in the year of 1856 in the newly Americanized and gold-burnished country of California, in the city of San Francisco, which stands on a narrow peninsula, about midway between either extreme of the mighty stretch of western seaboard, beside a bay unequalled by any along the whole seven thousand miles of shore line, and unsurpassed as a harbor by any in the world.

California was then a-weary. Young, strong, with untouched, undreamed of resources a thousand-fold more dazzling than any yet uncovered, with a million matchless years before her during which to turn and overturn the world's great centres of civilization, penetrate the mysteries of time, and bring to pass the unknowable, she was a-weary, spiritless, and suffering from that *tædium vitæ* which comes from excess.

Reaction after the flush times had fairly set in. Agriculture had not yet assumed great importance; still more insignificant were manufactures. Placer mining returns had fallen from an ounce of gold to half an ounce, then to a quarter of an ounce a day to the digger. Most of the merchants had already failed once, some of them several times.

There was little thought of mental culture at this time, of refinement and literature, or even of great wealth and luxury. The first dream was over of ships laden with gold-dust, and humbler aspirations claimed attention.

Slowly as were unlocked to man the wealth and mysteries of this Pacific seaboard, so will be the intellectual possibilities of this cradle of the new civilization. Civilization as the stronger element supplants savagism, drives it from the more favored spots of earth, and enters in to occupy. It is a fact no less unaccountable than pleasing to contemplate, that these western shores of North America should have been so long reserved, been held unoccupied so long. Constantinople shrivels, and San Francisco springs into being.

II

THE ATMOSPHERE

FTEN DURING THE progress of my literary labors,
questions have arisen as to the influence of California
climate and society on the present and future development of
letters. Charles Nordhoff said to me one day at his villa on the
Hudson,[1] "The atmosphere of California is so foreign to literary pursuits, the minds of the people so much more intent on
gold-getting and society pleasures than on intellectual culture
and the investigation of historical or abstract subjects, that your
isolation must have been severe. I could not help feeling this
keenly myself while on your coast. With a host of friends ready
to do everything in their power to serve me, I was in reality without companionship, without that broad and generous sympathy
which characterizes men of letters everywhere."

While it was true, I replied, that no great attempts were made
in the field of letters in California, and while comparatively few
of the people were specially interested in literature or literary
men, yet I had never experienced the feeling of which he spoke.

My mother used to say that she never felt lonely in her life;
and yet she was most companionable, and enjoyed society as
much as any one I ever knew. But her heart was so single and
pure, her mind so clear, intelligent, and free, that to commune
with her heart, and allow her mind to feed on its own intelligence, filled to the full the measure of her soul's requirements.

A healthy cultivated mind never can be lonely; all the universe is its companion. I never have experienced loneliness in my labors. If ever alone it was in an atmosphere of dead forms and conventionalisms crushing to my nature. Thus have I been lonely for my work, but not in it.

As for the public, I cannot say that I have ever felt any lack of appreciation on the part of the people of California. What chiefly has concerned me these twenty or thirty years has been, not what people were thinking of me and of my efforts, but how I could best and most thoroughly perform my task. To be free, free in mind and body, free of business, of society, free from interruptions and weariness, these have been my chief concern.

True, I could not overlook the fact that my motives were not fully understood nor my work appreciated. I had never expected very wide recognition or appreciation, and I always had more than I deemed my due. I did not regard my fate as resting wholly in the hands of the people of the Pacific coast; for unless I could gain the approval of leading men of letters throughout the world, of those wholly disinterested and most competent to judge, my efforts in my own eyes would prove a failure. Thus, from the outset, I learned to look on myself and the work, not as products of California, or of America, but of the world.

Perhaps men of letters are too critical; sensitive as a rule they always have been, though less so than men in some other professions. It is scarcely to be expected that the unappreciative masses should be deeply interested in such work. And as regards the more intelligent, each as a rule has something specially commanding his attention, which being of paramount interest to himself, he naturally expects it to command the attention of others.

Of what is called the culture of letters there was none during my working days in California. Grace Greenwood[2] adds to the social a physical reason why literature should not prosper in California. "I really cannot see how this coast can ever make a great record in scientific discoveries and attainments, and the loftier walks of literature—can ever raise great students, authors, and artists of its own. Leaving out of consideration the fast and furious rate of business enterprise, and the maelstrom-like force of the spirit of speculation, of gambling, on a mighty, magnificent sweep, I cannot see how, in a country so enticingly picturesque, where three hundred days out of every year invite you forth into the open air with bright beguilements and soft blandishments, any considerable number of sensible, healthy men and women can ever be brought to buckle down to study of the hardest, most persistent sort. I do not think California will ever be the rival of bleak little Massachusetts or stony old Connecticut in thorough culture, in the production of classical scholars, great jurists, theologians, historians, and reformers. The conditions of life are too easy. East winds, snows, and rocks are the grim allies of serious thought and plodding research, of tough brains and strong wills."

Says Walter M. Fisher, "As to the effects of the social climate of California on literary aspiration and effort, little that is favorable can be said for the present....California *père* is a *parvenu*, making money, fighting his way into society, having no time or taste for studying anything save the news of the day and perhaps an occasional work of broad humor. It is for his heir, California *fils*, to be a gentleman of leisure and wear 'literary frills.'"[3]

Oscar Wilde, upon returning from the Pacific coast in 1882, noted, "California is an Italy without its art. There are subjects for the artists; but it is universally true, the only scenery which inspires utterance is that which man feels himself the master of. The mountains of California are so gigantic that they are not favorable to art or poetry."[4]

In reality, if not called to consciousness by some external agent, the absorbed worker hardly knows or cares whether he occupies a tent in the wilderness or a parlor in the city. Nothing can exceed the satisfaction, if indeed congenial and comfortable, of a room in a country cottage, where the student may spread his books upon the floor, shut out superfluous light, and when weary, step at once into the warm glowing sunshine to stretch his limbs.

Change, almost always beneficial, to many is essential. Often many a one with an exquisite sense of relief escapes from the din and clatter of the city, and the harassing anxieties of business, to the soft sensuous quiet of the country, with its hazy light, aromatic air, and sweet songs of birds. Thus freed for a time from killing care, and reposing in delicious reverie in some sequestered nook, thought is liberated, sweeps the universe, and looks its maker in the face. No buzzing of business about one's ears; no curious callers to entertain. Safe with the world walled out, and heaven opening above and around. In the country the affections harmonize more with nature, engender purer thoughts, and develop lovelier forms than in the callous-shouldered unsympathetic crowds of a city.

As for the stone fences and east winds, I never knew them to be specially stimulating to brain work; no better, at all events, than the sand and fog of San Francisco, or the north winds and alternate reigns of fire and water in the valley of California. If to become a scholar it requires no discipline or self-denial greater than to withstand the allurements of her bewitching climate, California shall not lack scholars. When most ravished by the charms of nature, many students find it most difficult to tear themselves from work. Invigorating air and bright sunshine, purple hills, misty mountains, and sparkling waters may be enticing, but they are also inspiring.

With reference to the oft-repeated objections against the pursuit of wealth because of its influence on letters, much may be said. From necessary labor, and from the honorable and praiseworthy enterprise incident to life and independence, to an avaricious pursuit of wealth for the sake of wealth, the progress is so imperceptible and the change so unconscious that few are able to realize it. All nature covets power. Beasts, and men, and gods, all place others under them so far as they are able. Money is an embodiment of power; therefore all men covet money. Most men desire it with an inordinate craving wholly beyond its true and relative value. This craving fills their being to the exclusion of higher, nobler, and what would be to them, if admitted, happier sentiments.

This is the rule the world over; the passion is no stronger in California than in many other places. But it has here its peculiarities. Society under its present *régime* was begun on a gold-gathering basis. In the history of the world there never was founded so important a commonwealth on a skeleton so exclusively metallic. Three hundred thousand men and women came with no other object than to obtain gold and carry it away with them. Nor has the yellow ghost of this monetary ideal ever wholly abandoned the San Francisco sandhills.

The time will surely come in California when some will surfeit of wealth and hold the money struggle in contempt. They will tire of the harpies of avarice who snatch from them the mind-food for which they pine. Avarice is a good flint on which to strike the metal of our minds, but it yields no steady flame. The hope of sudden gain excites the passions, whets the brain, and rouses the energies; but when the effort is over, whether successful or otherwise, the mind sinks into comparative listlessness. It must have some healthier pabulum than cupidity, or it starves.

III

SPRINGS AND
LITTLE BROOKS

ERMONIZE AS WE may on fields and atmospheres, internal agencies and environment, at the end of life we know
little more of the influences that moulded us than at the beginning. In answer to that part of Mr Nordhoff's wonderings why I
left business and embarked in literature, I say I cannot tell. Ask
the mother why she so lovingly nurses her little one. Literature
is my love, a love sprung from my brain, no less my child than
the offspring of my body. There are those, says Hamerton,[1] "who
are urged toward the intellectual life by irresistible instincts, as
water-fowl are urged to an aquatic life."

There are millions of causes why we are what we are. That
my ancestors were of that stern puritan stock that delighted in
self-denial and effective well-doing, sparing none, and least of
all themselves, in their rigid proselytizing zeal, is another cause;
the hills and vales around my home, the woods and meadows
through which I roamed, my daily tasks—no pretence alone of
work—that were the beginning of a life-long practice of mental
and muscular gymnastics, were causes. Wrapped in the mysterious
enfoldings of fate are these innumerable springs of thought and
action, for the most part dormant till wakened by the sunshine
and storm wherein they bask and battle to the end.

My great-great-great-grandfather, John Bancroft, came from
London in the ship *James* in 1632. His descendants on my father's

side removed to Granville, Massachusetts, where my father, Azariah Ashley, was born in 1799, the fourth in a family of eleven.

My grandfather Azariah Bancroft was a man of good judgment, active in light open-air work, though not of sound health, for he was afflicted with asthma. My grandmother Tabitha Pratt was a woman of great endurance, tall and slender, with a facility for accomplishing work which was a marvel to her neighbors, clothing her large family with the wool and flax of her own spinning. The raw material entered the house from the farm, and never left it except as warm durable garments upon the backs of its inmates. My father said of his mother, "This was before the day of our country carding machines. My mother had nine operatives at this time, of different ages, and not a drone among us all. All were busy with the little picking machines, the hand-cards, the spinning-wheel, and the loom."

It seemed to me that boys in Ohio were early put to work, but they used to begin earlier in Massachusetts. A boy, or rather a baby of five, could ride horse to plow, a line for guiding the animal being then used less than at present. He could gather surface stones into little heaps, drop corn, and pull flax. During the next year or two, in his linen frock, he performed all kinds of general light work. After his seventh birthday my father was withdrawn from school during summer, his services on the farm being too valuable to be spared. In 1809 my grandfather Bancroft removed his family to Pennsylvania, where Yankees were then eyed suspiciously by the Dutch, and in 1814 he emigrated to Ohio.

As for my mother's side, the Howes, my great-great-grandfather, John Howe, was born in London in 1650, coming to New Haven, Connecticut, and there married at the age of sixty a girl of nineteen. They had a son, Ephraim Howe, Curtis Howe's father. Their descendants became scattered from the Atlantic to the Pacific.

Curtis Howe, grandfather of Hubert Howe Bancroft, from the Palmer family album, courtesy of The Bancroft Library (BANC PIC 1990.035 ALB)

My mother's father, Curtis Howe, was of singular mildness of disposition and singular firmness of character, and withal as lovable a nature as ever man had. He lived to the age of ninety-eight. The good man brought down heaven and made the world to him a paradise. As he advanced in years, my grandfather Curtis Howe had a growing desire to see all his children, making long journeys in his wagon rather than trust himself to a railway. So great was the desire to see his children in California that he finally summoned courage or faith sufficient to brave both railway and steam-ship, making the fatiguing, and for him dangerous passage by the Isthmus at the advanced age of ninety-four.

I was born in Granville, Ohio, on the fifth day of May, 1832. The town of Granville was settled by a colony from New England, and took its name from Granville, Massachusetts, whence many of its settlers came. It was in 1805 that a company was formed in Granville, Massachusetts, to emigrate to the far west, and two of the number went to search the wilderness for a suitable location. They selected a heavily timbered township in Ohio, in the county of Licking.

It was quite a different thing, this New England colony, from an ordinary western settlement. Though eminently practical, it partook rather of the subjective and rational element than of the objective and material. They with their households transplanted their opinions and their traditions, without abating one jot of either. With their ox teams and horse teams, with all their belongings in covered wagons, these colonists came, bearing in their bosoms their love of God, their courageous faith, their stern morality, their delight in sacrifice; talking of these things by the way, camping by the road side at night, resting on the Sabbath when all the religious ordinances for the day were strictly observed, consuming in the journey as many days as it now occupies half-hours, and all with thanksgiving, prayer, and praise.

Quite a contrast, this sort of swarming, to that which characterized the exodus to California less than half a century later, wherein greed usurped the place of godliness, and lust the place of love. Scarcely had the guns ceased braying that added to our domain the whole of Alta California when the chink of gold was heard upon our western seaboard, and thither flocked adventurers of every caste, good and bad, learned and unlearned, mercantile, mechanical, and nondescript. The sons of the puritans, in common with all the world, rose and hastily departed on their pilgrimage to this new shrine of Plutus. Here was a new departure in colonizing; nor yet a colonizing—only a huddling of humanity, drunk from excess of avarice.

Now it so happened that the farms of Azariah Bancroft and Curtis Howe adjoined. Both of these settlers were blessed with numerous children; both of my parents were born in 1799. My father was one of eleven, four boys and five girls reaching maturity. It was not the custom in that slow age for parents to shirk their responsibility. Luxury, pleasure, ease, had not yet usurped the place of children in the mother's breast; and as for strength to bear them, it was deemed disgraceful in a woman to be weak who could not show just cause for her infirmity. As I have said before, work was the order of the day—work, by which means alone men can be men, or women, women; by which means alone there can be culture, development, or a human species fit to live on this earth. Men and women, and boys and girls, all worked in those days, worked physically, mentally, and morally, and so strengthened hand, and head, and heart.

Thus working in the kitchen field and barn-yard, making hay and milking cows, reaping, threshing, spinning, weaving, Ashley Bancroft and Lucy Howe grew up. In the full course of time they were married, and had a hundred-acre farm of their own, and in time a two-story stone house and soon six children in it, of whom I was the fourth. My parents were married in Granville, Ohio, on the 21st of February, 1822; the 21st of February, 1872, at my house in San Francisco, they celebrated their golden wedding.

My father was what people in those days called a good boy, that is he was scarcely a boy at all—sober, sedate, pious, having in him little fun or frolic, though possessing somewhat of a temper. Before marriage my mother assisted her father from her own earnings in building his farm-house, and by further teaching and making bonnets of straw she accumulated enough for her wedding outfit. My father built residences and also built locks for the

Painting of Azariah Ashley Bancroft, the father of Hubert Howe Bancroft,
by L. Haus, courtesy of The Bancroft Library (19XX.500:042-FR)

Ohio canal. He wrote in his journal at age eighty-three, "During
the year 1840, while travelling south on business, I encountered
a fine rich farming country in Missouri, and in the following
year removed my family thither...; but after a sojourn of about
three years we were driven back by the unwholesomeness of the
climate. In 1850 I joined a company from Licking county bound
for California....I returned to Ohio in 1852. In 1861 I received

Painting of Lucy Howe Bancroft, the mother of Hubert Howe Bancroft,
by L. Haus, courtesy of The Bancroft Library (19XX.500:041-FR)

an appointment from the Government as Indian Agent for the
Yakima nation, at Fort Simcoe, where I remained for nearly four
years. I returned to San Francisco in November, 1864, and since
then have lived quietly and happily among my children and my
children's children."

While I am writing now in 1883, my father of eighty-five
is talking with my children, Paul, Griffing, Philip, and Lucy,

aged six, four, two, and one, respectively, telling them of things happening when he was a boy, which, were it possible for them to remember and tell at the age of eighty-five to their grandchildren, would be indeed a collating of the family book of life almost in century-pages. Living is not always better than dying; but to my boys I would say, if they desire to live long in this world they must work and be temperate in all things.

THUS IT HAPPENED that I was born into an atmosphere of pungent and invigorating puritanism, such as falls to the lot of few in these days of material progress and transcendental speculation. Planted in this western New England oasis, side by side with the piety and principles of the old Plymouth colony, and indeed one with them were all the antis and isms that ever confounded Satan—Calvinism and Lutheranism; abolitionism, once accounted a disgrace, later the nation's proudest honor; anti-rum, anti-tobacco, anti tea and coffee, anti sugar and cotton if the enslaved black man grew them, and anti fiddles and cushions and carpets in the churches, anti-sensualism of every kind, and even comforts if they bordered on luxury. Not only is religion, or the necessity of worship, as much a part of us as body, mind, or soul, but ingrafted superstition of some sort so fastens itself on our nature that the philosophy of the most skeptical cannot wholly eradicate it. I thank God for the safe survival of strict religious training; and I thank him most of all for emancipation from it. It may be good to be born in a hotbed of reverential sectarianism; it is surely better, at some later time, to escape it.

Excess of any kind is sure, sooner or later, to defeat its own ends. Take, for instance, the meetings inflicted on the society into which destiny had projected me. There were pulpit meetings, conference meetings, missionary meetings, temperance meetings, mothers' meetings, young men's meetings, Sunday-school meetings, inquiry meetings, moral-reform meetings, ministers' meetings, sunrise and sunset meetings, anti-slavery meetings, with extra impromptu meetings on special occasions. The consequence was that the young men of Granville were noted in all that region for their wickedness. The tender plant was so watered, and digged about, and fertilized, that natural and healthy growth was impeded. A distaste for theological discourse was early formed, arising, not from a distaste for religion, nor from special inherent badness, but from the endless unwholesome restraints thrown upon youthful unfoldings. "Born in sin!" was the cry that first fell on infant ears.

It is not to be wondered at that, after such an excess of piety and exalted contemplation, to the young elastic mind an interview with the devil was most refreshing; and as these boys were taught that in tobacco, small-beer, and the painted cards that players used, he lurked, there the pious urchins sought him. Clubs were formed—rough little knots—and meetings held for the purpose of acquiring proficiency in these accomplishments. Often after leaving our "inquiry" meeting—that is to say, a place where young folks met for the purpose of inquiring what they should do to be saved—have I gone home and to bed; then later, up and dressed, in company with my comrades I would resort to a cellar, garret, or barn, with tallow candle, cent cigars, and a pack of well-worn greasy playing-cards, and there hold sweet communion with infernal powers; in consequence of which enthusiasm one barn was burned and several others narrowly escaped burning. Strange to say, later in life, as soon as I learned how playing-cards were made, and that no satanic influences were employed in their construction or use, they ceased to have any fascination for me.

Now excess *per se* I hold to be the very essence of evil. We walk through life as on a tight-rope, and the more evenly we balance ourselves the better we can go forward. Too much leaning on one side involves a corresponding movement toward the other extreme in order to gain an equilibrium, and so we go on wriggling and tottering all our days. Hence, to avoid excesses of every kind I hold to be the truest wisdom.

THE PURITANS OF Granville called upon the benighted from all parts to come in and be told the truth. Likewise they comforted the colored race.

The most brilliant exploit of my life was performed at the tender age of eleven, when I spent a whole night in driving a two-horse wagon load of runaway slaves on their way from Kentucky and slavery to Canada and freedom—an exploit which was regarded in those days by that community with little less approbation than that bestowed by a fond Apache mother upon the son who brandishes before her his first scalp. The ebony cargo consisted of three men and two women, who had been brought into town the night before by some teamster of kindred mind to my father's, and kept snugly stowed away from prying eyes during the day. About nine o'clock at night the large lumber-box wagon filled with straw was brought out, and the black dissenters from the American constitution, who so lightly esteemed our glorious land of freedom, were packed under the straw, and some blankets and sacks thrown carelessly over them, so that outwardly there might be no significance of the dark and hidden meaning of the load. My careful mother bundled me in coats and scarfs, to keep me from freezing, and with a round of good-bys, given not without some apprehensions for my safety, and with minute instructions, repeated many times lest I should forget them, I climbed to my seat, took the reins, and drove slowly out of town.

Once or twice I was hailed by some curious passer-by with, "What have you got there?" to which I made answer as in such case had been provided. Just what the answer was I have forgotten.

I gave the inquirer no very reliable information; still, most of the people in that vicinity understood well enough what the load meant, and were in sympathy with the shippers. I was much nearer danger when I fell asleep and ran the wagon against a tree near a bank, over which my load narrowly escaped being turned. The fact is, this was the first time in my life I had ever attempted to keep my eyes open all night, and more than once, as my horses jogged along, I was brought to my senses by a jolt, and without any definite idea of the character of the road for some distance back. My freight behaved very well; once fairly out into the country, and into the night, the "darkies" straightened up, grinned, and appeared to enjoy the performance hugely. During the night they would frequently get out and walk, always taking care to keep carefully covered in passing through a town. About three o'clock in the morning I entered a village and drove up to the house whither I had been directed, roused the inmates, and transferred to them my load. Then I drove back, sleepy but happy.

Once my father's barn was selected as the most available place for holding a grand abolition meeting, the first anniversary of the Ohio State Anti-Slavery society. Rotten eggs flew lively about the heads of the speakers, but they suffered no serious inconvenience from them until after the meeting was over and they had begun their homeward journey. Beyond the precincts of the village they were met by a mob, and although spurring their horses they did not escape until the foul flood had drenched them. Those were happy days, when there was something to suffer for; now that the slavery monster is dead, and the slayers have well-nigh spent their strength kicking the carcass, there is no help for reformers but to run off into woman's rights, free-love, and a new string of petty isms which should put them to the blush after their doughty deeds. There are yet many souls dissatisfied with God's management of things, who feel themselves ordained to re-create mankind upon a model of their own. Unfortunately the model varies, and instead of one creator we have ten thousand, who turn the world upside down with their whimsical vagaries.

I CANNOT SAY THAT my childhood was particularly happy; or if it was, its sorrows are deeper graven on my memory than its joys. The fault, if fate be fault, was not my parents', who were always most kind to me. Excessive sensitiveness has ever been my curse; since my earliest recollections I have suffered from this defect more than I can tell. My peace of mind has ever been in hands other than my own; at school rude boys cowed and tormented me, and later knaves and fools have held me in derision.

How painful to a sensitive mind is the attention drawn by personal peculiarity. By nature I was melancholy without being morose, affectionate and proud, and keenly alive to home happiness and the blessings of every-day life. So far as I am able to analyze the failing, it arose from no sense of fear, inferiority, or vanity; it was simply a distaste or disinclination to feel obliged to meet and converse with strangers when I had nothing to see them for, and nothing to converse about; at the same time, when urged by duty or business, my mind once made up, I could go anywhere and encounter any person without knee-shaking. A simple invitation to a general assemblage oppressed my spirits, yet I would go and endure from a sense of duty. I was timid; others were bold. I would not subject myself to the withering influences of their loud and burly talking. With the natural desire for approbation mingled a nervous horror of shame; with aspirations to excel, the fears of failure; and I felt a strong repugnance to exposing myself at a disadvantage, or permitting such merit as I possessed to be undervalued or over matched by the boisterous and contemptible. Yet I would contend that it was less pride than a morbid excess of modesty curdled into a curse.

E. B. Lytton,[2] the author of *Caxtoniana*, says in his essay on shyness: "When a man has unmistakably done a something that is meritorious, he must know it; and he cannot in his heart undervalue that something, otherwise he would never have strained all his energy to do it. But till he has done it, it is not sure that he can do it." Without theory, without knowing or caring what was the cause, all through my younger days to meet people was distasteful to me; so I threw round myself a wall of solitude, within which admittance was gained by few. This state of things continued until some time after I had arrived at the age of maturity, when it gradually left me; enough remaining, however, to remind me of the past. It is one of the saddest processes of life, this of tanning the heart and turning the seat of the affections into a barb-proof ball.

And thus it was that later in life, as I wandered among the scenes of my childhood, sadness stood everywhere prominent. I seemed to remember only the agony of my young life, and every step I took wrung from my very soul tears of sympathetic pity. The steed well fed and warmly housed at night will stand the keenest, coldest day unflinchingly; give the boy a happy life, and the man will take care of himself. Let him who will, after arriving at maturity, defy opinion and the contempt of the world, but do not ask the child to do it. Nothing exceeds the misery suffered by the sensitive youth from the jeers of companions. Let the boy be a boy during his youth, and as far into manhood as possible. I was reared in that saturnine school which teaches it to be a sin for the insulted boy to strike back; and often in my school-days, overwhelmed with a sense of ignominy and wrong, I have stolen off to weep away a wounded spirit. The fruit of such training never leaves the child or man.

Yet for all that, and more, of puritan Granville I may say, it was well for this man that he was born there.

MY BOYHOOD WAS spent in working during the summer, and in winter attending school, where I progressed so far as to obtain a smattering of Latin and Greek, and some insight into the higher mathematics. However, no sooner had my father placed in a forward state of cultivation his hundred acres, built a large stone house, and cleared the place from debt, than, seized by the spirit of unrest, he sold his pleasant home and moved the family to the swamps of New Madrid, Missouri. After three years of ague in that sand-blown land, we all packed ourselves back and began where we left off, but minus the comfortable stone house and farm. Child as I was, the earliest and most determined ambition of my life was to work and earn the money to buy back the old stone house.

Call it discontent, ambition, enterprise, or what you will, I find this spirit of my father fastened somewhat upon his son. It is characteristic of some people that they are never satisfied except when they are a little miserable. Often in the simple desire for new companionship we tire of unadulterated good, and communion with some sorrow or the nursing of some heartache becomes a pleasing pastime. There are persons who will not be satisfied, though in their garden were planted the *kalpa-tarou,* the tree of imagination, in Indian mythology, whence may be gathered whatever is desired.

After all, this spirit of unrest, of discontent, is the spirit of progress. Underlying all activities, it moves every enterprise; it is the mainspring of commerce, culture, and indeed of every agency that stimulates human improvement. Nay, more: that fire which may not be smothered, that will not let us rest, those deep and ardent longings that stir up discontent—is it any other influence than Omnipotence working in us his eternal purposes, driving us on, poor blind cogs that we are in the wheel of destiny, to the fulfillment of predetermined ends?

The stone house in Granville, Ohio, that Azariah Ashley Bancroft built
(*above:* historic photo courtesy of the Granville Historical Society;
below: contemporary photo courtesy of Chris McDonald)

LOVELY LITTLE GRANVILLE! dear, quiet, home-nook; under the long grass of thy wall-encircled burial-ground rest the bones of these new puritan patriarchs, whose chaste lives, for their descendants, and for all who shall heed them, bridge the chasm between the old and the new, between simple faith and soul-sacrificing science, between the east and the west—the chasm into which so many have haplessly fallen.

I well remember, on returning from my absence, how the villagers came out of their houses to stare at me; and the old stone house, how rusty, and rugged, and mean it looked compared with the radiance my unhackneyed brain clothed it in. Never is there a home like the home of our youth; never such sunshine as that which makes shadows for us to play in, never such air as that which swells our little breasts and gives our happy hearts free expression, never such water as the laughing dancing streamlet in which we wade.

IV

THE COUNTRY BOY
BECOMES
A BOOKSELLER

≈

CROSSING A MUDDY street one rainy day on her way to school, my eldest sister, dark-eyed and tender of heart, encountered a sandy-haired but by no means ill-looking youth who made way for her by stepping back from the plank which served pedestrians. Of course these two young persons fell in love, and in due time were married. And in this rain, and mud, and marriage, I find another of the causes that led me eventually to embark in literature. The marriage took place in 1845, when I was thirteen years of age, and the happy couple made their home in Geneva, New York, where Mr Derby was then doing business. Subsequently he removed his bookstore and family to Buffalo.

Mingled with my school and Sunday duties, interspersed with occasional times for shooting, fishing, swimming, skating, sleighing, and nut and berry gathering, was work, such as grinding bark, sawing wood, chopping, clearing, fencing, milling, teaming, ploughing, planting, harvesting, and the like, wherein I could take but little interest and make no progress, and which I most heartily hated.

To my great delight, a year or so after the marriage of my sister, I was offered the choice of preparing for college or of entering the Buffalo bookstore. The doctrine was just then coming into vogue that in the choice of a profession or occupation youthful proclivities should be respected, but the youth should not be coerced. This, within the bounds of reason, is assuredly the correct idea.

The two courses in life at this time offered me were each not without attractions, and for a time I hesitated, thinking that if I adopted one it would be well, and if I adopted the other it would be better. To have the elements of success within is the main thing; it then does not import so much in what direction they are developed. It matters little what one does, it matters everything how one does it. To be a good brick-maker is infinitely better than to be a bad book-maker.

This marriage of my sister changed the course not only of my own destiny but of that of every member of my family. It was the hinge on which the gate swung to open a new career to all of us. Puritan Granville was a good place to be reared in, but it was a better place to emigrate from. It was in the world but not of the world. Success there would be a hundred acres of land, a stone house, six children, an interest in a town store or a grist-mill, and a deaconship in the church.

But how should I decide the question before me? What had I upon which to base a decision? Nothing but my feelings, my passions, and propensities—unsafe guides enough when coupled with experience, but absolutely dangerous when left to shift for themselves.

Study had always strong fascinations for me, and the thought of sometimes becoming a great lawyer or statesman set heart and head rapturously a-twirl. I am told that I was quick to learn when young, and that at the age of three years I could read the New Testament without having to spell out many of the words. If that be true, the talent must have ended with my childhood, for later on taking up study I found it almost impossible to learn, and still more difficult to remember, whatever talent I may have possessed in that direction having been driven out of me in the tread-mill of business.

One winter I was sent to the brick school-house. There presided over the boys at one time my mother's brother. The Howes engaged in school teaching naturally, they and their children, boys and girls, without asking themselves why. They were good teachers, and they were good for nothing else. Take from them their peculiar knack of imparting knowledge and there were left only bones and nerves kept in motion by a purposeless brain. The one who taught in Granville had written a grammar, and all the boys were compelled to study it. It consisted chiefly of rules which could not be understood and contained little of the kind of examples which remained fastened in the mind to be afterward of practical value.

Those Howe grammar lessons were the curse of that winter. Often I wept over the useless and distasteful drudgery, but in vain. Tears were a small argument with my parents where they deemed duty to be concerned; and the brother made my mother believe that if I failed in one jot of his grammar, there would be no hope for me afterward in any direction. Mathematics I enjoyed. Stretched on the hearth before a blazing fire, with book and slate, I worked out my problems during the long evenings, and then took the Howe grammar lesson as I would castor-oil.

My studies were mixed with house and barn duties, such as paring apples, pounding rusk, feeding and milking the cows, and scores of like occupations. Long before daylight I would be called from my slumber to work and study, a summons I usually responded to with alacrity. But still the Howe grammar hung over all my joys like a grim shadow, darkening all delights. For, in that I did not love the grammar, the Howe did not love me, and he made the place exceedingly uncomfortable, until finally my mother became satisfied that I was injudiciously and unfairly treated, and to my great joy took me from the purgatory.

I was passionately fond of music, not so much of listening as performing. The intensest aspirations of my life seem to have taken this form; I longed to do rather than to enjoy. Purposeless pleasure was not pleasant to me. To-day I find neither satisfaction nor profit in reading or writing, or doing anything for my own personal enjoyment. There must be an aim, and a high, immediate, and direct one, if in my doing or being I am to find pleasure.

To return to the matter of choosing between study and business. Finding myself possessed of these and many other burning aspirations, without stopping to count the cost, childlike I struck at once for the prize. If self-devotion and hard study could win, it should be mine. So I chose the life of a student, and spent another year in preparing for college. There was an academy as well as a college in the place; indeed, my native town, in its way, was quite a seat of learning.[1]

It was now the winter of 1847–8, and bravely I set about my self-imposed task, studying hard, and for a time making fair progress. I was still obliged to work morning and evening and during the vacations, with now and then a holiday. I was much alone in my studies, although I attended my teacher as zealously as if I had been under competitive influence. My nearest and indeed almost the only companion I had at this time was my cousin Edgar Hillyer, afterward United States judge for Nevada. In age he was a year my senior, but in ability and accomplishments many years. He was a good student, nimble on the violin, and a jolly companion. He aided and influenced me more than any other in many things. When he entered college, I was left alone. Still I toiled on, but before the time for entering college arrived I had lost somewhat of my interest in study; without the stimulus of sympathizing friends and competition, the unfed fire of my ambition died away.

Meanwhile Mr Derby had made occasional visits to my father's house, and in listening to his conversation I became attracted toward Buffalo. There was, moreover, in me a growing desire for independence; not that I was dissatisfied with my home so much as with myself. I longed to be doing something that would show results; I wanted to be a man, to be a great man, to be a man at once. The road to learning was slow and hard; besides, my father was not rich, and although ready to deny himself anything for me, I could see that to continue my plan of study would be a heavy tax on him. Yet I loved it, and, as the sequel will show, left it here only to take it up at a future time. Now I wanted money, not to love and cherish as a thing admirable in itself, but as a servant to do my bidding, as an Aladdin lamp to buy me independence, leisure, culture.

Mine must be a fruitful life. And at the portal of every ambition, even of intellectual ambition, stands money. But there is such a thing as too much money. Too much wealth leads to a loss of time, of heart, of head—the only true wealth. Get money, but get it only in order that you may ransom mind, for it is mind and not money that makes the man.

Thus unsettled in my mind by the allurements of active business and city life, my attention distracted from studies, discontented in the thought of plodding a poverty-stricken path to fame, and unwilling to burden my father for a term of years, I asked and obtained leave to enter the shop, selling books, for the nonce, offering stronger attractions than studying them. Nor am I now disposed to cavil over the wisdom of my final decision. Commercial and industrial training offers advantages in the formation of mind, as well as scientific and literary training. In regard to education, there is too much teaching from books and too little from nature. Early training should be such as teaches how to learn, rather than an attempt to acquire knowledge. This done, every hour of life thereafter will be a garnering of knowledge. Hence if I might have another chance at life, with my present ideas I would pay the most careful attention to three things: I would need all the powers within me to learn how to think, how to write, and how to speak, for I could then command myself and others.

ABOUT THE 1ST of August, 1848, I left Granville for Buffalo, where I arrived on the 9th. I was now sixteen years of age, and this may be regarded as my starting out in life. Then I left my father's house, and ever since have I been my own master, and made my own way in the world. There was no railway from my native town, and my journey was made in a canal-boat as far as Cleveland, and thence by steam-boat over Lake Erie to Buffalo. Permission was given to me to ride horse on the towpath in lieu of paying fare.

The bookseller's shop was the largest establishment I had ever seen, and the, to me, huge piles of literature, the endless ranges of book-shelves, all filled me with awe. A day or so was spent in looking about the city. On the Monday following my arrival I was put to work in the bindery and initiated into the mysteries of the book business. I underwent a vast amount of unpalatable though doubtless very necessary training, till the bindery was sold. I was then left in an uncertain state, with nothing in particular to occupy me. After being given plainly to understand by my brother-in-law that my person was not at all necessary to his happiness, I was finally thrust into the counting-house at the foot of the ladder, as the best means of getting rid of me.

The fact is, I was more ambitious than amiable, and my brother-in-law was more arbitrary than agreeable. I was stubborn and headstrong, impatient under correction, chafing over every rub against my country angularities; he distant, unsympathizing, and injudicious in his management of me. I felt that I was not understood, and saw no way of making myself known to him. Any attempt to advance was frowned down, not because he hated, or wished to injure me, but because he thought boys should not be presumptuous, that they should be kept in the background— especially pale, thin, thoughtful, super-sensitive brothers-in-law.

For some six months I held this anomalous position, till one day the chief book-keeper intimated to me that, in the opinion

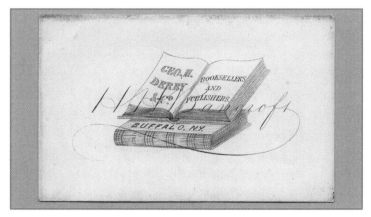

Business card of H. H. Bancroft while selling books for George Derby of Buffalo, courtesy of The Bancroft Library (BANC MSS 73/64 v.1:06)

of the head of the house, nature had never designed me for a bookseller—a species of divinity in the eyes of these men born but not made—and that, should I retire from active duty, no one about the premises would be overwhelmed with sorrow. In plain English, I was discharged.

I now determined to start in business of my own account. Since I could not work for the Buffalo bookselling people, I would work for myself. I borrowed enough to take me back to Ohio, and Mr Derby, it appears, had sufficient confidence to trust me for a few cases of goods. I hurried to Granville for a horse and wagon, loaded up, and began distributing my goods among the country merchants. For about four months I travelled in this manner over different parts of my native state, selling, remitting, and ordering more goods, and succeeding in the main very well; that is to say, I paid my expenses, and all the obligations I had before contracted, and had enough left to buy a silver watch, and a suit of black broadcloth. Never was watch like that watch, fruit as it was of my first commercial earnings.

Winter approaching, I sold out my stock, paid my debts, and went home. Owing to my success, it seems, I had risen somewhat in the estimation of the Buffalo book magnates, and just as my mind was made up to enter school for the winter I was summoned back to Buffalo, with instructions to bring my youngest sister, Mary, afterward Mrs Trevett. We reached Buffalo on the 8th of December, 1849. This time I was to enter the store as a recognized clerk, and was to receive a salary of one hundred dollars a year from the first of January, 1850.

I now began to look upon myself as quite a man. I relaxed a little from puritanical ideas of propriety. I bought a high hat and a cane; smoked now and then surreptitiously a cigar; a gaudy tie adorned my neck, and a flashy ring encircled my finger. I do not think I ever held myself in higher estimation before or since; at no time of my life did I ever presume so much on my knowledge, or present personally so fine an appearance.

Honored and trusted, my moroseness evaporated at intervals. Soon I found myself more in sympathy with my employer, and felt that he now began somewhat to understand me. And here I will pay my tribute of respect to the memory of George H. Derby. His death I felt more keenly than that of any other man who died. He was among the best friends I ever had—he, and his wife, my sister. He held his own peculiar views regarding the training and treatment of relatives. He seemed to delight in squeezing and tormenting, in a business way, all who were in any wise allied to him by blood or marriage, and the nearer the relationship the greater the persecution. Of a didactic turn in all his relations, he was particularly severe with me. Yet he seemed to repose the utmost confidence in me, trusted me, a green boy in the midst of the whirlpool of the Californian carnival, with property which he could ill afford to lose, the risk being regarded as little less than madness on his part by business acquaintances. His goodness will remain fresh in my memory to my dying day.

With a sister ever kind to me, and an employer really desirous of advancing my best interests, the training I underwent at

H. H. Bancroft as a young man, courtesy of The Bancroft Library
(Bancroft, Hubert Howe—POR1)

this period of my life was about as injudicious for an ambitious, sensitive youth as could well have been devised. Even after my return from Ohio I was at times headstrong, impatient of restraint, impudent, angry, and at open war with my brother-in-law; yet I was eager to learn, quick, and intelligent, and would gladly have worked, early and late, with faithful and willing diligence in any advancing direction. But it seemed that my employer still considered it best for me to be kept down; to be censured much and never praised; to have one after another placed above me. The consequence was that during the greater part of my stay in Buffalo I was in a sullen state of mad exasperation. I was hateful, stubborn, and greatly to be blamed, but the discipline I received only intensified these faults. One word of kindness, and I would have followed this man to the death. I know he was full of generous feeling for me even while I tried him most; for when, after leaving for California, I sent him a letter, opening my heart as I had never done before, on receipt of it, as my sister told me, he threw himself upon the sofa and wept like a child.

I fell into my own ways, which were very bad ways; tramping the streets at night with jovial companions, indulging in midnight suppers, and all-night dancings. Lo, how the puritan's son has fallen! Conscience pricked faithfully at first. I soon grew easier in mind; then reckless; and finally neglecting my Bible, my prayers, and all those Sabbath restraints which hold us back from rushing headlong to destruction, I gave myself over to hardness of heart. Yet all this time I usually listened with enjoyment and profit to one sermon on Sunday; I also attended lectures given by Park Benjamin, G. P. R. James, Gough, and others; these and novel-reading comprised my intellectual food.[2]

Into that bookseller's shop I went with all the untempted innocence of a child; out of it I came with the tarnish of so-called manly experience. There I plucked my first forbidden fruit from the tree of knowledge of good and evil; yet the sense of right remained, and that remorse which ever mixes bitter with the sweets of sin. The inherent morality doctrine, and a trusting to it, is flattering, but exceedingly risky. Men and women, young and old, inherently good or inherently bad, nine times in ten will stand or fall according to environment, according to influence, temptation, companionship.

Every now and then I would turn over a new leaf; bravely begin a diary, scoring the first page with high resolves, such as total abstinence from every species of wickedness, tea, coffee, wine, tobacco; determined to think, speak, and do no evil, to walk always as before the eye of Omniscience, clean in heart, pure in mind, and strong in body. Sometimes I would keep my diary up during the year; then again I would open a blank book, without fixed dates, and discharge my burning thoughts into it in the hope of relief. No sooner had I departed from Buffalo on my way to California than all desire left me to commit these foolish boyish excesses. There was then no one to hoodwink, no watchful eye to circumvent; it ceased to be amusing when I was my own master; so when thrown into the pandemonium at San Francisco I had not the slightest inclination to make a beast or a villain of myself.

But the time thus lost! How have I longed to live again the former three years and the three following. Six years of my young life as good as squandered, in some respects worse, for instead of laying the foundation of health, purity, intellect, I was crushing my God-given faculties, damming the source of high thoughts and ennobling affections, and sowing by Stygian streams the wild seeds of perdition.

It was a few months before I left my home for the first time that gold had been discovered in California; but not until a year later did the news so overspread the country as to cause any excitement in the quiet town of Granville. Scarcely had I reached Buffalo the second time when letters informed me that my father was thinking of going to the new El Dorado. The ancient leaven of industry and enterprise still worked in him, and although far past the average age of those who joined the pilgrimage to the golden shrine, he could not resist the temptation. Though but little over fifty, he was called an old man in those days in California. By the 1st of February it was settled that he would go, and in March, 1850, he set sail from New York. I had a boyish desire to accompany him, but did not think seriously of going at the time. I was more absorbed in flirtations, oyster suppers, and dancing parties than fascinated by the prospect of digging for gold.

Nevertheless, the wheel of my destiny was turning. In January, 1851, Mr Derby received a letter from an uncle of mine, my mother's brother, then in Oregon, ordering a large quantity of books. This demand, coming from a new and distant market, made quite an impression upon the mind of the ardent young bookseller, Derby. Visions filled his brain of mammoth warehouses rising in vast cities along the shores of the Pacific, of publication offices and manufacturing establishments, having hundreds of busy clerks and artisans, buying, making, and selling books. He would walk the floor excitedly and talk of these things by the hour, until he was well nigh ready to sell out a safe and profitable business, pack up, and go to California himself. These visions were prophetic; and through his instrumentality one such establishment as he had dreamed of was planted in the metropolis of this western seaboard, although he did not live to know of it.

My nearest companion at this time was a fellow-clerk, George L. Kenny, the son of an Irish gentleman. He had come to seek his fortune in America, and found his way almost direct from the mother country to the Buffalo bookstore, where he had been engaged but a few months when I first arrived there. From that day for over a third of a century his life and mine have been closely linked.[3]

Mr Derby was a man of many ideas. Though practical and conservative in the main, the fertility of his brain and his enthusiasm

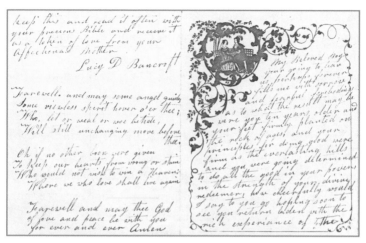

Letter from H. H. Bancroft's mother upon his leaving for California,
courtesy of The Bancroft Library (BANC MSS 73/64 BOX 1:20)

often gave him little rest. Once seized with the thought of California in connection with his business, he could not dispossess his mind of it. Finally he talked more directly of me as the one to go—why I do not know, unless it was that I could best be spared, and also that I had friends there, who, if they succeeded, might supply me with money. Oregon was the point at this time talked of. I was ready to go, but had as yet no special enthusiasm for the adventure.

Meanwhile Mr Derby had ventured three shipments of goods to the Pacific; one small lot sold at seventy-five per cent above the invoice, and although the other two were lost, one by fire and the other by failure of the consignee, the one success was sufficient to excite great hopes. This, together with a letter from my father received toward the latter part of December, 1851, determined me to go to California. I was anxious to have Mr Kenny accompany me. He would like much to go, he said, but had not the money. I urged him to speak to Mr Derby about it. He did so, when our now most gracious employer replied: "For a long time I have been desirous of your going to California; only I would not propose it." He then entered heartily into our plans and opened the way for both of us.

I felt by no means eager for gold; it was rather boyish adventure that prompted me. California was pictured in my mind as a nondescript country on the other side of huge mountains, which once overstepped, with most that I cared for left behind, there was little hope of return. I was not so weaned but that I must see my mother before I departed, perhaps never to return; and although it involved an unpleasant and expensive journey over the snow in the dead of winter, I immediately performed it.

Then bidding all a long farewell, and calling on the way upon Mr James C. Derby of Auburn, my comrade Kenny and I went down to New York, entered our names at the Irving house, and were ready to embark by the next steamer.

V

HAIL CALIFORNIA!
ESTO PERPETUA!

Never despair; but if you do, work in despair.
—Burke

S O LARGE A portion of the Californian's life, during the first twenty years following the discovery of gold, was occupied in the passage by the various routes from one side of the continent to the other, that a picture of that epoch, with this prominent and characteristic scene left out, would be unfinished. During the first fifteen years of my residence on the western coast I made the passage between New York and San Francisco by way of Panamá no less than eleven times, thus spending on the water nearly one year, or what would be almost equivalent to every other Sunday during that time. Many made the voyage twice or thrice as often; life on the steamer was but a part of California life. It was there the beginning was made; it was sometimes the ending. It was there the excrescences of egotism and the morbid superfluities fastened on the character by local training, or lack of training, first began the rub against the excrescences and superfluities of others, all of which tended to the ultimate polish and perfection of the mass.

In my *California Inter Pocula* I have given a full account of the voyage out. I shall not therefore repeat the description here, but merely say that on the 24th of February, 1852, in company with Mr Kenny, I embarked at New York on the steamer *George*

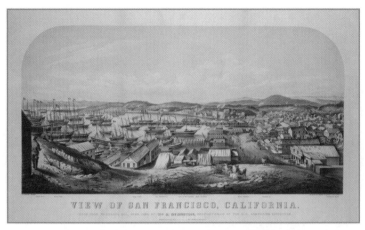

VIEW OF SAN FRANCISCO, CALIFORNIA.

View of San Francisco from Telegraph Hill, April 1850,
lithograph by F. Palmer, N. Currier, W. B. McMurtrie,
courtesy of The Bancroft Library (1963.002: 1495-FR)

Law, bound for Habana. On reaching this port the sixth day,
passengers, mails, and freight were transferred, with those of
the steamer from New Orleans, to the *Georgia*, which that night
sailed for Chagres, touching at Jamaica. Arrived at Chagres we
were sent into Aspinwall to disembark, so as to ride over some
six or eight miles of the Panamá railway just then opened for that
distance. After the usual delay on the Isthmus we embarked on
the steamer *Panamá* the 12th of March, touched at several ports
on the Pacific, and reached San Francisco at twelve o'clock the
first day of April.

When I arrived in California John Bigler was governor.
The capital had just been removed from Vallejo to Sacramento.
In San Francisco the wars with squatters, Peter Smith titles, and
water-lot frauds were attracting the chief attention.[1] Portions of
the streets were brilliantly lighted from the glare of gambling-
saloons; elsewhere all was thick darkness. There was no system
of street lights, and in the dark places about the docks, in the back
streets, and round the suburbs, many dark deeds were committed.

Crime, driven into holes and hiding-places by the Vigilance Committee of 1851, was beginning to show its face again.[2] Agriculture was attracting more attention than at any time previous. Bull and bear fights at the Mission were in vogue. Gambling was somewhat on the decline—times were becoming too hard to risk a hundred dollars for an evening's amusement—but it was the day of grand raffles, grand auction sales, grand quartz-mining schemes, and Biscaccianti concerts.[3] Fire and flood held their alternate sway over the destinies of town and country, aiding other causes to accomplish business disruptions and failures.

It was the day of long annual sessions of the legislature, of fighting officials, and anti-Chinese meetings—though concerning this last named fermentation the question arises, When in California was it not?[4] The most striking feature of the town at night to a stranger was the gambling-houses, the more aristocratic establishments being then situated on the plaza[5] and Commercial

PUBLISHED BY CHARLES P. KIMBALL, NOISY CARRIER'S PUBLISHING HALL.
LONG WHARF, SAN FRANCISCO, CALIFORNIA.

Long Wharf, lithograph by C. Kimball, c. 1856,
courtesy of The Bancroft Library (1963.002: 0073-A)

street, and the lower dens principally on Long wharf. The better class supported a fine orchestra of five or six wind instruments, while in others a solitary cracked piano or violin squeaked the invitation to enter. The building was usually a mere shell, while the interior was gorgeously decorated and illumined with chandeliers presenting a mass of glittering glass pendants. During week-days these places were usually quiet, but at night and on Sundays the jingling of coin and the clinking of glasses were mingled with the music of the orchestra in hellish harmony.

Round the table sat beautiful females in rustling silks and flaming diamonds, their beauty and magnificent attire contrasting strangely with the grizzly features, slouched hats, and woolen shirts of their victims. The license for a single table was fifty dollars per quarter. There were hundreds of saloons, so that the revenue to the city was large.

Two days and nights amid scenes like these in San Francisco were sufficient to drive away the little wit left by the strange experiences at Habana, on the Isthmus, and on board the steamers, and to properly prepare the boyish mind for the pandemonium of the miners. The two days were spent by me in wandering about the business parts of the town, wading muddy streets, and climbing sand-hills; the nights in going from one gaming-house to another, observing the crowds of people come and go, watching the artistic barkeepers in their white coats mixing fancy drinks and serving from gorgeously decorated and mirrored bars fiery potations of every kind, gazing in rapt bewilderment upon the fortune-turning table with its fatal fascinations, marking the piles of money increase and lessen, and the faces behind them broaden and lengthen, and listening to the music that mingled with the chinking of gold, the rattling of glasses, and the voices of rough, loud-laughing men. "There are indeed but very few," says Addison, "who know how to be idle and innocent." Two days and nights of this; then from Long wharf we boarded a steam-boat and went

Five riverbed miners,
courtesy of The Bancroft Library (1905. 16242:079-CASE)

to Sacramento. Sacramento seemed to offer more attractions for
the opening of a small shop than any other place. San Francisco
was the larger field, but it seemed more than fully occupied, as
has been the case in every city and town on the coast from the
beginning.

Sacramento having been decided on as the more fitting field,
the next thing was to write Mr Derby and inform him of our
decision. This done we took the boat for Marysville, *en route*
for Long bar,[6] in search of my father. There I was initiated into
the mysteries of mining and mining life. The placer diggings of
this locality were then good, and so remained for several years,
but the population changed every few months, the dissatisfied
leaving and new adventurers coming in. Ten dollars a day was
too little in the eyes of those accustomed to make twenty, and so
they sold or abandoned their claims and prospected for richer
diggings. Wandering thus from placer to placer for years, they

lost their opportunity, if not their lives, and usually ended their mining career where they began, without a dollar.

When my father came to the country, my eldest brother, Curtis, who had preceded him, was keeping a store and hotel at Long bar. He was doing well, making money steadily and safely. At one time he had five thousand dollars surplus capital, with which he started for San Francisco, there to invest it in city lots. Had he done so, buying judiciously and holding, he might now be worth millions instead of nothing. Unfortunately, on his way he communicated the plan to John C. Fall, then one of the leading merchants of Marysville, and high in the esteem of my brother. By him he was induced to make a venture which involved his leaving Long bar, and ultimately ended in financial ruin. My brother erected a building at Rich bar, on Feather River, and there opened a hotel and store.

For a time all went well. Up and down the river the diggings were rich, and gold dust was poured into his coffers by the quart. The establishment at Long bar seemed insignificant in comparison, and being attended with some care, he sold it and moved his family to Rich bar. My father remained at Long bar. He had been in the country now about two years, had accumulated quite a little sum, and contemplated soon returning home. But shortly before setting out an opportunity offered whereby he might increase his little fortune tenfold, and without a risk of failure—so it seemed to him and to others.

Quartz mining was about this time attracting attention, and the prospect was flattering. But the cost of extracting was more than had been anticipated, and the methods of saving the gold after the rock was crushed were imperfect.

Two miles from Long bar, near the Marysville road, was a place called Brown valley, and through this ran a quartz ledge, long known but regarded as valueless, because no one could extract the gold from the hard white rock which held it. When, however, quartz mining became the fashion, new companies staked off claims to the ledge. One of these companies was called the Plymouth, always a pleasing name to the ear of my father, and he was induced to invest.

I found my father in connection with other members of the Plymouth association, busily engaged in working this mine. He occupied a little cloth house in the vicinity of the ledge, and being the owner of a good mule team, he employed himself in hauling rock from the mine to the mill, about one mile apart, and in gathering wood with which to burn the rock, so that it could be the more easily crushed. The first night I spent with him in the hotel at Long bar. Foremost among my recollections of the place are the fleas, which, together with the loud snorings and abominable smells proceeding from the great hairy unwashed strewed about on bunks, benches, tables, and floor, so disturbed my sleep that I arose and went out to select a soft place on the hill-side above the camp, where I rolled myself in a blanket and passed the night, my first in the open air of California.

The next day found me settled down to business. As eight or nine months must elapse before my letter from Sacramento could be received by Mr Derby, and goods reach me by way of Cape Horn, it was arranged that I should work with my father for the Plymouth company. In the morning we climbed the oak trees scattered about the valley, and with an axe lopped off the large brittle branches, adding them to the already huge pile of wood beside the mill. At noon we proceeded to the little cloth house, unharnessed and fed the animals, and then cooked and ate our dinner. Beefsteak, beans, bread, and potatoes, with coffee, canned fruits, pancakes, or anything of the kind we chose to add, constituted the fare of self-boarding miners in those days; but with all our culinary talents we could not offer Mr Kenny a meal sufficiently tempting to induce him to partake of it, and so he obtained his dinner from a boarding-house near by, and left shortly afterward for Rich bar.

I cannot say that I enjoyed this kind of life, and could scarcely have endured it but for the thought that it was only temporary. At night the animals were turned loose to graze. Early in the morning, long before the sun had risen, I was up and over the hills after them. Stiff and sore from the previous day's work, wet with wading through the long damp grass, I was in no humor to enjoy those glorious mornings, ushered in by myriads of sweet songsters welcoming the warm sunlight which came tremblingly through the soft misty air. To the clouds of top-knotted quails, the leaping hare, the startled deer, and thick beds of fragrant flowers, I was indifferent. The music of the mules alone allured me. How I loaded and lashed the poor dumb beasts in my distemper. The sharp rock cut my hands, the heavy logs of wood strained my muscles; and my temper, never one of the sweetest, fumed and fretted like that of a newly chained cub. I never took kindly to misfortune; prosperity fits me like a glove. It is good to be afflicted; but I do not like to receive the good in that way. I will admit that adversity may be good for other people, but the continuance of prosperity has never by any means been prejudicial to me, either in mind or morality.

The night before leaving Buffalo I had danced until morning. It happened that about the only clothes saved from the thieves of the Isthmus were the ones used on that occasion. These I wore until work turned them into rags. In the pocket I one day found a pair of white kid gloves, relic of past revelries, and putting them on I gathered up the reins, mounted the load, and beating my mules into a round trot, rode up to the mill laughing bitterly at the absurdity of the thing. It was the irony of gentlemanly digging. Ten or twelve loads was a fair day's work; I hauled twenty or twenty-five. I had brought plenty of books with me, but could not read, or if I did it was only to raise a flood of longings which seemed sometimes to overwhelm me. My soul was in harmony with nothing except the coyotes which all night howled discordantly behind the hills.

After two months of this life the hot weather was upon us. Water was becoming scarce. We had heaped up the wood and the rock about the mill, but the mill did not pay. There was always something wrong about it.

Skepticism is a plant of slow growth. I cannot tell why neither my father nor I should have seen by this time that the enterprise was a failure. But we did not see it. We had schooled ourselves in the belief that the rocky bank contained a mint of money which must some day enrich the possessor. But there was then nothing more to be done, and my father concluded to pay a parting visit to my brother at Rich bar and set out for home. For our work we took more shares, and still more in exchange for the team and the scattering effects, and abandoned it all forever. Several years afterward I learned that a new company had taken possession of the claim and was doing well. Not long after leaving the place I became convinced that the enterprise was a failure, and firmly resolved that thenceforth, whatever speculation I might at any time engage in, it should be not with my own labor. I might stake money, but if I worked with my hands I would have pay for such labor.

Behold us now! my old father and me, tramping over the plains beneath a broiling sun about the middle of June, each with a bundle and stick, mine containing my sole possessions. In the early morning, fresh from sleep, with gladness of heart at leaving the beautiful valley of hateful occupation behind, we marched away over the hills at a round pace. By noon the sun poured its most effectual wrath. My feet blistered; my limbs

Hard Road to Travel, lithograph by Britton and Rey,
courtesy of The Bancroft Library (1963:002:0027 A)

ached. Thinking over my short experience in the country and
my present position, I exclaimed, "If this be California, I hope
God will give me little of it."

That day we walked thirty miles. I persuaded my father to
camp that night. The next day we travelled in the cool air of the
Sierra. The third day we reached Rich bar. My father, after a
visit of about a week, returned with the express train—of mules,
not steam-cars—to Marysville, where he took the boat for San
Francisco, and thence the steamer homeward.

As I had still six months or thereabout to wait for my goods,
I agreed to remain with my brother Curtis for such compensation
as he should choose to give. My duties were to carry on the store
and look after the business generally in his absence. Mr Kenny
was likewise engaged by my brother in an establishment carried
on by him at Indian bar, a few miles down the river. There we
remained until November, when we went to San Francisco.

Shortly before leaving Rich bar I had received intelligence of the death of Harlow Palmer, who had married my sister Emily in Buffalo. Her husband was among the noblest of men. I said nothing to any one; but I wandered beside the river to weep alone.

This was only the beginning of sorrow. Scarcely had I reached Sacramento when the death of George H. Derby was announced. The two brothers-in-law had both been swept away by the cholera the same month. I wandered about the quagmires and charred remains of the city—for Sacramento had about that time been visited by both flood and fire—the miry and sombre surroundings according well with the despond-sloughs and ashen contemplations within. All my plans and purposes I saw at once were at an end. I knew very well that no one else, now that Mr Derby was dead, would do so foolish a thing as to continue shipments of goods to an inexperienced moneyless boy in California.

Having no further business in the burned-out mudhole of Sacramento, I went down to the bay and put up at the Rassette house.[7] Kenny was with me. I was determined, whatever the cost, that Mrs Derby should have the full amount of the invoice, with commissions added, as soon as the goods could be converted into money and the proceeds remitted to her. I determined there should be no sacrifice, even if I had to peddle the stuff from door to door. I began to look about for employment till the goods should arrive. At none of the several book and stationery shops in town was there any prospect. I was thin, young, awkward, bashful, had no address, and was slow of wit. I explained the poverty of my prospects and declared the purity of my intentions. All was in vain; nobody would have my services.

Mr Kenny was more fortunate. He was older than I, and possessed of an Irish tongue withal; he made friends wherever he went. A partnership was offered him by William B. Cooke, established at the corner of Merchant and Montgomery streets. The terms were that Kenny should place upon Cooke's shelves

"List of Valuable Books for Sale by H. H. Bancroft & Geo. L. Kenny, Sac.," 1852, courtesy of The Bancroft Library (PFZ1036B119)

the stock sent me; that the proceeds should be remitted east as fast as sales were made. I must shift for myself; but this did not trouble me.

Well, the goods arrived, and the firm of Cooke, Kenny, and Company was organized. Everything went on satisfactorily, and the whole amount was remitted to the executors of Mr Derby's estate. I greatly preferred remaining in the city altogether. Mines and the miners, and country trading of any kind, had become exceedingly distasteful to me. I felt, if an opportunity were offered, that I would prove competent and faithful in almost any capacity; for though diffident I had an abundance of self-conceit, or at least of self-reliance, and would do anything. Accustomed to work all my life, idleness was to me the greatest of afflictions. My bones ached for occupation, and I envied the very hod-carriers.

Thus for six months, day after day, I tramped the streets of San Francisco, seeking work, and failed to find it. Thousands have since in like manner applied to me, and remembering how the harsh refusals once cut my sensitive nature, I try to be kind to applicants of whatsoever degree, and if not always able to give work I can at least offer sympathy and advice. Finally, sick with disappointment, I determined to leave the city. The choice must be made quickly, for the last dollar from Rich bar was gone, and I would not live on others, or run in debt with nothing wherewith to pay. My future turned upon a hair.

In the spring of 1853 the San Francisco papers began to notice a new town on the California northernmost shore of the Pacific, Crescent City. On both sides of the boundary line between Oregon and California were extensive mining districts. Knowing of no better place, I determined to try my fortune at Crescent City; so, with fifty dollars borrowed, and a case of books and stationery bought on credit, I embarked on board the steamer *Columbia* about the middle of May. Two days and one night the voyage lasted—long enough to leave me on landing completely prostrated with sea-sickness and fatigue. Taken ashore, I crawled to a hotel and went to bed.

Adjoining the hotel was the general merchandise store of Crowell and Fairfield, and there I made the acquaintance of Mr Crowell, which resulted in mutual confidence and esteem. At

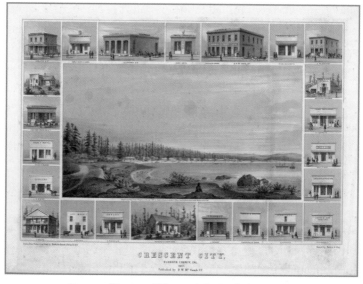

Crescent City, 1857, lithograph by Kuchel & Dresel,
courtesy of The Bancroft Library (1963.002:0902-D)

length, he made me an offer of fifty dollars a month to keep his
books, with the privilege of placing my stock on his shelves and
selling from it for my own account free of charge. As I slept in
the store, indulged in little dissipation, and was not extravagant
in dress, my expenses were very light, while the profits on my
goods, which I sold only for cash, were large. As the business
augmented, my salary was increased. However, some six months
later the firm failed. Being dissatisfied with my life there, I disposed
of the business, built a one-story brick store, which I leased to
some hardware merchants, and leaving my affairs in the hands
of an agent I went down to San Francisco.

Life at Crescent City was in most respects similar to life in
the mines. There was the same lack of virtuous women, the same
species of gaming-houses, drinking saloons, and dens of pros-
titution. A ranchería of natives occupied the northern horn of

the Crescent, and with them the mild-mannered citizens of the town endeavored to live in peace. One night the ranchería took fire. The natives thought the white men wished to burn them out, and the white men began to fear the red men intended to overturn everything. Morning, however, threw light upon the matter. It appears a drunken man had taken lodgings in a native hut, and built a fire of wood against the bark boards of the house. The pioneer citizens of the Crescent were orderly. They could not therefore silently pass by the affront cast on their dusky neighbors by an unworthy member of their own color; and in the absence of a court of law they held a court of inquiry, followed by a court of retort, requiring the vile white man to fully satisfy them for loss and damage to their property, and then to leave the place.

The two and a half years I spent at Crescent City were worse than thrown away, although I did accumulate some six or eight thousand dollars. With an abundance of time on my hands, I read little but trashy novels, and though from my diffidence I did not mingle greatly with the people, I improved my mind no better than they at cards or billiards. On Sundays there was horse-racing, or foot-racing, or cock-fighting; and often a band of rowdies would make the night rounds, pounding at every door, and compelling the occupant to administer drink to all. During my residence there, I made several trips on business to San Francisco and on the whole managed my affairs with economy. I well remember the first five hundred dollars I made.

MY SISTERS HAD often urged me strongly to return to the east. My brick store was now worth eight thousand dollars, and rented for two hundred and fifty dollars a month, sufficient to make me comfortable without work. Often have I thought how fortunate it was that I did not start in business at San Francisco or Sacramento at that time, since the inevitable result would have been failure. As I have said, almost every firm then doing business failed; and if men with capital and experience, with a large trade already established, could not succeed, how could I expect to do so? In November, 1855, with Mr Pomeroy as a companion, I sailed from San Francisco for New York.

VI

THE HOUSE OF
H. H. BANCROFT
AND COMPANY

Seest thou a man diligent in business, he shall stand before
kings; he shall not stand before mean men. —Proverbs

HOME AGAIN! None but a wanderer, and a youthful wanderer, can feel those words in their fullest import. Out of
the depths and into paradise. Away from harassing cares, from the
discordant contentions of money-getting, from the contaminations of filthy debaucheries, beyond the shot of the pistol or reach
of bowie-knife, safe home, there let me rest. And how the men,
and women, and children all eyed me; one saying, "You are not a
bear," and another, "I do not see but that you look very like other
people." The impression seemed to prevail at the east in those
days that a Californian could not be otherwise than brown and
bearded, and rough and red-shirted.

I found my sister Mrs Derby, with her three daughters, cosily
keeping house in Auburn, New York. My youngest sister, Mary,
was with her. Soon Mrs Palmer, my second sister, came down
from Buffalo to see her Californian brother. I tried my best to
like it at the east, to make up my mind to abandon California
and settle permanently in Buffalo or New York, to be a comfort
to my sisters, and a solace to my parents; but the western coast,
with all its rough hardships and impetuous faults so fascinating,

had fastened itself too strong upon me to be shaken off. And so round many a poor pilgrim California has thrown her witcheries, drawing him back to her bright shores whenever he attempted to leave them.

Suddenly in April, 1856, I made up my mind no longer to remain there. I had visited enough and wasted time enough. I was impatient to be doing. There was that in California which harmonized with my aspirations and drew forth energies which elsewhere would remain dormant.

On one side of the continent all was new, all was to be done; on the other side beginnings were pretty well over. To the satisfied and unambitious an eastern or European life of *dolce far niente* might be delicious; to me if I had millions it would be torment. I must be something of myself, and do something by myself; it is the Me, and not money, that cries for activity and development.

"One thing do for me," said my sister, "and you may go."

"I will; what is it?"

"You remember the money sent from California in return for goods shipped by Mr Derby? The money is now so invested that I am fearful of losing it. Help me to get it, then take it and use it in any way you think best."

"I will help you to get it," said I, "most certainly, but I could not sleep knowing that your comfort depended on my success. I may be honest and capable, and yet fail. I may woo fortune but I cannot command her. The risk is altogether too great for you to take."

"Nevertheless I will take it," replied my noble sister, and in that decision she decided my destiny.

How a seemingly small thing, as we have before remarked, will sometimes turn the current, not only of a man's own future life, but that of his friends, his family, and multitudes who shall come after him. In this womanish resolve of my sister—womanish because prompted by the heart rather than by the head—the destinies of many hundreds of men and women were wrapped.

By it my whole career in California was changed, and with mine that of my father's entire family. Herein is another cause, if we choose to call it so, of my embarking in literature.

Now I determined to execute the original plan formed by Mr Derby. I would establish at once a credit, for without that my capital would not go far, and plant myself in San Francisco with aspirations high and determination fixed.

A Mr John C. Barnes had been a warm friend of Mr Derby and was partner in a larger stationery house in New York. I stated to him my plans, and received the assurance that everything possible should be done to forward my wishes. I wanted to establish business relations with the leading publishers of the east.

California credit in New York at that time rated low. Nearly every one I met had lost, some of them very heavily, either by flood, or fire, or failure. Some of their customers had proved dishonest, others unfortunate, and a curse seemed attached to the country from which at one time so much had been expected. I told them I was starting fresh, untrammelled, with everything in my favor, and I believed I could succeed. At all events, I begged the merchants to see Mr Barnes about my worthiness. The consequence was that when I called the second time almost every one was ready to sell me all the goods I would buy. From that day my credit was established, becoming firmer with time, and ever afterward it was my first and constant care to keep it good.

OCTOBER 1856 SAW me again *en route* for San Francisco. I found Mr Kenny occupying his old store with a small stock of goods. I told him to settle his business and come with me, and he did so. We engaged the room adjoining, near the corner of Merchant and Montgomery streets, where ten years before a yerba-buena bordered sand-bank was washed by the tide-waters of the bay. Our stock arriving shortly after in good order, we opened it and began business under the firm name

Montgomery Street, San Francisco, lithograph,
courtesy of The Bancroft Library (1963.002:0618-A)

of H. H. Bancroft and Company about the first of December, 1856. During those months, the inside was exposed to the weather while the building was taking on a new front; but in such a climate this was no hardship. At night we closed the opening with empty boxes, and I turned into a cot bed under the counter to sleep; in the morning I arose, removed the boxes, swept the premises, put the stock in order, breakfasted, and was then ready to post books, sell goods, or carry bundles, according to the requirements of the hour. We let two offices, thus reduced our rent one third, the original sum being two hundred and fifty dollars a month. Mr Kenny was a salesman; he had already a good trade established.

Times were exceedingly dull. Year after year the gold crop had diminished or required twice the labor and capital to produce former results. Business depression was far greater than at any time since the discovery of gold. But hard times are the very best of times in which to plant and nourish a permanent business. Hard times lead to careful trading and thrift; flush times to recklessness and overdoing. On every side of us old firms were falling to pieces, and old merchants were forced out of business.

Toward the end of the first year the idea struck me that I might use my credit further, without assuming much more responsibility, by obtaining consignments of goods in place of buying large quantities outright. But this would involve my going east to make the arrangements, and, as Mr Kenny would thus be left alone, I proposed to Mr Hunt, whose acquaintance had ripened into friendship, to join us, contribute a certain amount of capital, and take a third interest in the partnership. The proposition was accepted. Mr Hunt came into the firm, the name of which remained unchanged, and soon after, that is to say in the autumn of 1857, I sailed for New York. My plan was successful. I readily obtained goods on the terms asked to the amount of sixty or seventy thousand dollars, which added largely to our facilities.

Before returning to California, which was in the spring of 1858, I visited my parents, then living as happily as ever in Granville. My views of life had changed somewhat since I had left my boyhood home, and later they changed still more. I was well enough satisfied then with the choice I had made in foregoing the benefits of a college course, and my mind is much more clear upon the subject now than then.

Were a boy of mine to ask me to-day, "Shall I enter college?" I should inquire, "For what purpose? What do you intend to do or to be? Are you satisfied with your position and possessions, or shall you desire fame or wealth?" It is one thing to make money and quite another to be made by money.

WHILE STOPPING IN Buffalo once more I made the acquaintance of Miss Emily Ketchum, daughter of a highly respected and prominent citizen of the place, and of whom my sister Mrs Palmer was loud in praise. Her face was not what one would call beautiful, but it was very refined, very sweet. She was tall, with light hair and eyes, exquisitely formed, and very graceful. Her mind was far above the average female intellect, and well cultivated; she was exceedingly bright in conversation, and with a ready wit possessed keen common-sense. Her well trained voice in singing was one of the sweetest I ever heard. I was captivated and soon determined to marry her—if I could. My time was short; I must return to my affairs immediately. We had not met half a dozen times before I called one afternoon to say good-by. She was entirely unconscious of having aroused any special interest in me and as a matter of course I could not then make a proposal.

What to do I did not know. I could not leave matters as they were and go back to California to be absent perhaps for years, and yet I could not speak my heart. I dared not even ask if I might write, lest I should frighten her. At last fortune came to my relief. The young woman had lately become deeply interested in religion, was a new convert, as she said, though her whole life had been one of the strictest religious training. Naturally she was keen for proselytes, and evidently took me for a heathen, one of the worst sort, a California heathen. Zealously she attacked me, therefore, her eyes sparkling, her cheeks glowing, her whole soul lit with inspiration in proclaiming the blessedness of her faith. I listened attentively; I could have listened had she been demonstrating a problem in Euclid, or talking of Queen Victoria's new bonnet. After a three hours' session, during which by dropping here and there a penitent word, the fire of her enthusiasm had been kept ablaze, I rose to take my leave.

"Absorbed in business as I am," I said, "away from home and its hallowing influences, worship is neglected and piety grows cold. Had I you to remind me of my duty now and then, I might do better."

"Would that I could be of such assistance to you," she replied. "You can."

"How?" she asked.

"Write me occasionally."

"I will," was the prompt response.

It was enough, more than I had expected, better than I could have hoped for: I had her promise to write—little cared I what she wrote about—and then, of course, I could write to her. My heart was light, the barrier of conventionalism was broken.

Nor did I forget her sermon. I remembered it on the railway journey to New York; I remembered it on the steamer deck, down in the tropics, as I gazed up into the starlit sky and thought of her and her sweet words. And I vowed to be a better man, one more worthy of her. I remembered it when on reaching San Francisco I put my brains in my pocket and joined the good people of Calvary church in their march heavenward. I remembered it at the Sabbath-school where I taught, at the prayer-meetings which I attended. All through the religious life which for the next ten years I so strictly led I never forgot her, for she was with me, with her holy living and that dear love and fond devotion of which in part she robbed God to bestow on me.

In truth I was earnest in my profession both of love and of godliness; and my love was crowned with success, for I married Emily Ketchum. In the spring of 1859 I again visited the east, and in the autumn of that year my marriage took place, which was in this wise: The sacred correspondence had long since been cut off. To the parents the device was altogether too transparent. On reaching Buffalo I immediately presented myself and found the lady amiable and tractable. I told her I had come to marry her; in reply she declared herself willing, but feared her parents would object to her going so far from them. That night I left for Ohio, to give time for consideration. In three weeks I returned and asked her if she was ready. For herself, yes, but she would not leave her father and mother without their full and free assent; so to the father and mother I went. They sighed and hesitated;

Emily Ketchum Bancroft with daughter Kate,
from the album *The Founding of a Family*, courtesy of
The Bancroft Library (BANC MSS 73/64 C. V.1)

I desired a 'yes' or 'no,' and receiving neither that night I left for
New York. This time I remained away six weeks, and on returning,
all was happiness. In due time the ceremony was performed and
we sailed for California. The first two years we lived on Harrison
street, between First and Second streets, and there my daughter
Kate was born. Afterward we passed certain seasons at Oakland
and Alameda.

THE HOUSE OF H. H. BANCROFT AND COMPANY • 65

I WILL ONLY GLANCE over the leading events of the next twelve years, and hasten to the subject-matter of this book. Shortly after my return to San Francisco, to make room for the large additions to our stock, we rented two rooms fronting on Merchant street, in the rear of our store, cutting through the partition wall to give us access from the Montgomery-street store. Subsequently we occupied the whole building on Merchant street, forty by sixty feet, three stories. Meanwhile, though little more than a boy myself, I gave special attention to my boys. I was determined that my establishment should be a model of order, morality, and discipline. At once studying them and teaching them, of some I made salesmen, of others book-keepers, giving to the brightest and most devoted leaderships.

In 1860 my father was appointed by President Lincoln as Indian agent in Washington territory, and took up his residence at Fort Simcoe. My mother soon joined him, and also my youngest sister, Mary, who afterward married Mr T. B. Trevett. After the expiration of the term, four years, my parents settled in San Francisco, and Mrs Trevett in Portland, Oregon.

Having now an abundance of means at my command, I determined to establish a branch in the stationery business among the wholesale houses, as we had little of that trade. The political sky darkened; then roared rebellion; and for the next five years fortunes were thrust on Californian merchants from the rise in gold, or rather from the depreciation of the currency in which they paid their debts—fortunes which otherwise could never have been accumulated but by generations of successful trade.

In January, 1862, my wife made a visit to her friends at home, and the following summer I took a hurried trip to London, Paris, New York, and Buffalo, bringing her back with me. This knocking about the world, with the time which it forced from business devoted to observation and thought under new conditions, was a great educator. It was then that ambition became fired, and ideas came rushing in on me faster than I could handle them. Notwithstanding I had read and studied somewhat, yet the old world, with its antique works and ways, seen by the eye of inexperience, was at once a romance and a revelation. In 1866–7 I spent a year in Europe with my wife, made the tour of Great Britain and the continent, and came back to Buffalo. There we remained the following winter, visited Washington in the spring, and returned to San Francisco in the autumn of 1868.

Meanwhile the business had assumed such proportions that more room was absolutely necessary. I succeeded in obtaining seven lots together, three on Market street and four on Stevenson street, making in all a little more than seventy-five by one hundred and seventy feet.[1] This was regarded as far beyond business limits at the time, but it was the best I could do, and in six or seven years a more desirable location could not be found in the city.

It was one of the turning-points of my life, this move to Market street. Had I been of a temperament to hasten less rapidly; had I remained content to plod along after the old method, out of debt and danger, the map of my destiny would present quite a different appearance. The truth is, my frequent absence from business had weaned me from it—this, and the constantly recurring question which kept forcing itself on my mind, "Is he not worse than a fool who labors for more when he has enough; worse than a swine who stuffs himself when he is already full?" If I could turn my back upon it all, it would add to my days, if that were any benefit. Had I known what was before me I would probably have retired from business at the time, but in my employ were as fine a company of young men, grown up under my own eye and teachings, as ever I saw in any mercantile establishment, and I had not the heart to break in pieces the commercial structure which with their assistance I had reared, and turn them adrift upon the world.

In Europe, for the first time in my life, I had encountered a class of people who deemed it a disgrace to engage in trade. Many I had seen who were too proud or too lazy to work, but never before had come to my notice those who would not, if they could, make money, though it involved no manual labor. Here the idea seemed first to strike me, and I asked myself, Is there then in this world something better than money that these men should scorn to soil their fingers with it? I never yet was ashamed of my occupation, and I hope never to be; otherwise I should endeavor speedily to lay it aside. Nor do I conceive any more disgrace attached to laboring with the hands than with the head. The consuming of my soul on the altar of avarice I objected to, not work. I have worked twice, ten times, as hard writing books as ever I did selling books. But for the occasional breaking away from business, long enough for my thoughts to form for themselves new channels, I should have been a slave to it till this day, for no one was more interested and absorbed in money-making while engaged in it than I.

In accordance with my purposes, then, historical and professional, in 1869 I began building. Already I had in contemplation a costly dwelling, parts of which had been constructed in England and at the east, and shipped hither from time to time, till a great mass of material had accumulated. Soon a hundred men or more were at work.

And now began a series of the severest trials of my life, trials which I gladly would have escaped in death, thanking the merciless monster had he finished the work which was half done. In December, 1869, my wife died. Other men's wives had died before, and left them, I suppose, as crushed as I was; but mine had never died, and I knew not what it was to disjoin and bury that part of myself. It is not a very pleasant sensation, that of being entirely alone in the universe, that of being on not very good terms with

H. H. Bancroft with daughter Kate, c. 1865,
from the album *The Founding of a Family*,
courtesy of The Bancroft Library
(BANC MSS 73/64 C. V.1)

the invisible, and caring little or nothing for the visible. True, I
had my little daughter; God bless her! but when night after night
she sobbed herself to sleep upon my breast, it only made me angry
that I could not help her.

O God, snatch my love not from me ere I have scarcely tasted
it! For her who so lately clung to me as to an anchor of safety to
be as by rude hands hurried hence seemed not heavenly to me.
Not until the fire lighted by disease had spent itself and the fever
heat had fled, leaving the heart still and the limbs cold, did love
forsake the glazing eye, or those fleshless fingers cease to press
the clasped hand.

She is gone, and who cares? Neither deities nor men. The world laughs, and swears, and cheats as hitherto. The undertaker's long face of mercenary solemnity haunts you; the hustling crowd, careless of your cankering grief, maddens you. There is no doubt that a well balanced mind is the best remedy against afflictions, but great grief often throws mind out of balance, so that, the remedy being absent, the application fails.

The burden of my loss was laid upon me gradually; it was not felt in its fullest force at first; it was only as the years passed by that I could fully realize it. Occupation is the antidote to grief; give me work or I die, work which shall be to me a nepenthe to obliterate all sorrows. And work enough I had, but it was of the exasperating and not of the soothing kind. If I could have shut myself up, away from the world, and absorbed my mind in pursuit of whatever was most congenial to it, that would have been medicine indeed. It was building and business, grown doubly hateful now that she for whom I chiefly labored had gone. I stayed the workmen on the house, and let it stand, a ghastly spectacle to the neighborhood for over a year; then I finished it, thinking it well enough to save the material. The carpenters still hammered away on the store building, and completed it in April, 1870.

The business was now one of the most extensive of the kind in the world. It was divided into nine departments, each in charge of an experienced and responsible head. Thus far it was purely a mercantile and publishing house. To make it perfect, complete, and symmetrical, manufacturing must be added. This I had long been ambitious of doing, but was prevented by lack of room. Now this obstacle was removed, and I determined to try the experiment. The mercantile stock was brought up and properly arranged on the first and second floors and basement. On the third and fourth floors respectively were placed printing-office and bookbindery. Several small establishments were purchased and moved into the new premises, such as a printing, an engraving, a lithographing,

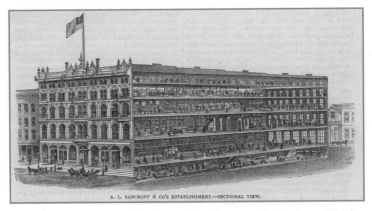

A. L. BANCROFT & CO'S ESTABLISHMENT.—SECTIONAL VIEW.

Cutaway of H. H. Bancroft's San Francisco literary industry. *Paper World*, March 1881 (vol. 2, no. 3). Courtesy of The Bancroft Library (E13.B23.C6)

and a stationery establishment. A steam-engine was placed in the basement to drive the machinery above, and an artesian well was dug to supply the premises with water. A department of music and pianos was also added.

My library of Pacific coast books was alphabetically arranged on the fifth floor. Then I changed the name of the business, the initial letters only, my responsibility, however, remaining the same.[2] The idea was not eminently practicable, I will admit, that I should expect to remain at the head of a large and intricate business, involving many interests and accompanied by endless detail, and see it continue its successful course, and at the same time withdraw my thoughts and attention from it so as to do justice to any literary or historical undertaking. "How dared you undertake crossing the Sierra?" the pioneer railroad men were asked.

"Because we were not railroad men," was the reply.

THUS, I FELT, was ended the first episode of my life. I had begun with nothing, building up by my own individual efforts, in sixteen years, a mammoth business of which I might justly feel proud. I had schooled from the rudiments, and carried them through all the ramifications and complications of that business, a score and more of active and intelligent young men, each competent to take the lead in his department, and of them I was proud. Arrived at that estate where money-making had ceased to be the chief pleasure, I might now retire into idleness, or begin life anew.

But this was not to be. I must first pay the penalty of over-doing, a penalty which in my business career I have oftener paid than the penalty arising from lack of energy. The business extended from British Columbia to Mexico, and over to the Hawaiian islands, Japan, and China, and was in a flourishing condition.

Woes, however, were at hand. First appeared one following the opening of the Pacific railway. This grand event was celebrated with guns, and banners, and music, as if the millennium had come; and every one thought it had. There were many afterward who said they knew and affirmed it at the time that this road at first would bring nothing but financial disaster and ruin to California, but before such disaster and ruin came, I for one heard nothing of its approach. Every one wanted to sell, and could not, and there was a general collapse.

Business was likewise revolutionized. Immediately the railway was in running order, the attention of buyers throughout the country, large and small, was turned toward the east. "We can now purchase in New York as well as in San Francisco," they said, "and save one profit." Consequently prices in San Francisco fell far below remunerative rates. Many merchants failed.

More was yet to come. As all Californians well know, the pros-perity of a season depends on the rainfall. As if to try the endur-ance of our merchants to the utmost, three dry winters and five long years of hard times followed the opening of the railway.[3] That my business did not fail, with such an accumulation of untoward circumstances, proved conclusively that it was sound and well managed.

It may easily be seen that to draw one's mind from business at such a time and fix it on literary pursuits was no easy matter. Cares, like flies, buzz perpetually in one's ears; lock the door, and they creep in through invisible apertures. Yet I attempted it, though at first with indifferent success. The work on the fifth floor, hereinafter to be described, was not always regarded with favor by those of the other floors. It drew money from the business, which remaining might be the means of saving it from destruction. Would it not be better to wait till times were better, till money could be spared, and danger was passed?

Yet I persisted. Day after day, and year after year, I lavished time and money in the vain attempt to accomplish I knew not what. It was something I desired to do, and I was determined to find out what it was, and then to do it if I could. Although my mind was in anything but a condition suitable for the task, I felt in no mood to wait. My age—thirty-seven or thereabout—was somewhat advanced for undertaking a literary work of any magnitude, and no time must be lost. I did not consider it right to bring disaster on others, but I never believed that such a result would follow my course. True, it is one thing to originate a business and quite another to maintain it; yet I felt that the heads of departments were competent to manage affairs, reporting to me every month. So I toiled on with greater or less success, oftentimes with a heavy heart and a heated brain, tired out, discouraged, not knowing if ever I should be permitted to complete anything I had undertaken, in which event all would be lost. It was between the hours of work that I experienced the greatest depression; once at my table and fairly launched upon my writing, I was absorbed by it, and forgot for the time the risks I was taking.

This season of trial was not without its benefits. It forced upon me a species of self-abnegation which I might never otherwise have attained. Had pleasure been pleasurable to me; had I been able to enjoy high living and extravagant expenditures with my affairs in so uncertain a state, or had my finances been such as to enable me without stint to enjoy gentlemanly leisure, or literary or other idling, it is doubtful whether I could have mustered courage and persistence to carry forward my undertaking. One knows not what can be done or suffered until necessity makes the demand. In time, however, the clouds cleared; the wheels of business revolved with smoothness and regularity; my work assumed shape; part of it was finished and praised; letters of encouragement came pouring in like healthful breezes to the heated brow; I acquired a name, and all men smiled upon me. Then I built Babylonian towers, and climbing heavenward, peered into paradise.

VII

FROM BIBLIOPOLIST
TO BIBLIOPHILE

≈

THUS FAR, ALL through life, had my intellectual being craved ever more substantial nutriment. While in business I was Mammon's devotee; yet money did not satisfy me. Religion tended rather to excite longings than to allay them. Intellectual cultivation implies thinking, and thinking tends to weaken faith. I could not understand it then, but I see it clearly now. It was the enlargement and ennoblement of the immaterial Me that I longed for. Often I asked myself, Is this then all of life? to heap up merchandise for those who come after me to scatter, and to listen on Sundays to the reiteration of dead formulas? Insatiable grew my craving, and I said I will die to the past, to money getting, to station rooting; I will unlock the cage of my thoughts and let them roam whithersoever they will. To be at all fitted for writing history, or indeed for writing anything, a man must have at his command a wide range of facts which he stands ready to regard fairly and to handle truthfully. And so it was that, as time and my work went on, I found within me stronger and ever increasing the desire of independent and exact thinking.

While in Europe and elsewhere every moment of my spare time was occupied in historical reading and in the study of languages; yet it seemed like pouring water into a sieve. The appetite was ravenous, increased by what it fed on. Books! books! I revelled in books. After buying and selling, after ministering to others all my life, I would now enjoy them; I would bathe my mind in them till saturated with the better part of their contents.

I read and crammed my head with basketfuls of facts and figures, only to crowd them out and overflow it with others. Hundreds of authors I skimmed in rapid succession until I knew or felt I knew nothing. Then I threw aside reading for a time and let my thoughts loose, only to return again to my beloved books.

Had my mind been able to retain what it received, there would have been greater hope of filling it. The activities and anxieties of trade had left me unprepared all at once to digest this great and sudden feast. As I have before said, only a trained mind possesses the power of pure abstraction. It seemed to me I had no memory for isolated or individual facts. For many months all seemed chaotic, and whatever was thrown into my mental reservoir appeared to evaporate, or become nebulous, and mingle obscurely with the rest. While in Buffalo, after my return from Europe, I wrote somewhat; but the winter was spent under a cloud, and it was not until after a trip to New York and Washington, and indeed a longer one to San Francisco, where I was forced to pause and reflect, that the sky became bright and my mental machinery began to work with precision. The transition thus accomplished was like the ending of one life and the entering upon another, so different and distinct are the two worlds, the world of business and the world of letters.

In an old diary begun the 5th of May, 1859, I find written: "To-day I am twenty-seven years of age. In my younger days I used to think it praiseworthy to keep a diary. I do a great deal of thinking at times; some of it may amount to something, much of it does not. I often feel that if I could indulge, to the fullest and freest extent, in the simple act of discharging my thoughts on paper, it would afford my mind some relief."

To BEGIN AT the beginning. In 1859 William H. Knight, then in my service as editor and compiler of statistical works relative to the Pacific Coast, was engaged in preparing the *Hand-Book Almanac* for the year 1860. From time to time he asked of me certain books required for the work. It occurred to me that we could probably have frequent occasion to refer to books on California, Oregon, Washington, and Utah, and that it might be more convenient to have them all together. I always had a taste, more pleasant than profitable, for publishing books, for conceiving a work and having it wrought out under my direction. To this taste may be attributed the origin of half the books published in California during the first twenty years of its existence as a state, if we except law reports, legislative proceedings, directories, and compilations of that character. By having all the material on California together, so that I could see what had been done, I was enabled to form a clearer idea of what might be done in the way of book-publishing on this coast. Accordingly I requested Mr Knight to clear the shelves around his desk, and to them I transferred every book I could find in my stock having reference to this country. I succeeded in getting together some fifty or seventy-five volumes. This was the origin of my library, sometimes called the Pacific Library, but latterly the Bancroft Library. I looked at the volumes thus brought together, and remarked to Mr Knight, "That is doing very well; I did not imagine there were so many."

I thought no more of the matter till some time afterward, happening in at the antiquarian bookstore of Epes Ellery, my eyes lighted on some old pamphlets, and it occurred to me to add them to the Pacific coast books over Mr Knight's desk. This I did, and then examined more thoroughly the contents of other shops all about town. Frequently I would encounter old books in auction stores, and pamphlets in lawyers' offices, which I immediately bought and added to my collection. The next time I visited the east, I secured from the second-hand stores and bookstalls of New York, Boston, and Philadelphia, whatever fell under my observations.

Bibliomaniac I was not. This, with every other species of lunacy, I disliked. I know nothing morally wrong for one possessing the money, and having an appetite for old china, furniture, or other relics, to hunt it down and buy it; but it is a taste having no practical purpose in view, and therefore never would satisfy me. So in books; to become a collector, one should have some object consistent with usefulness. It is true that thus far, and for years afterward, I had no well defined purpose, further than the original and insignificant one, in gathering these books; but with the growth of the collection came the purpose.

And the *rationale* of it? Ask a boy why he fills his pockets with marbles of different varieties, and his answer will be, "To see how many kinds I can get." After all, what are any of us but boys?

I had a kind of purpose at the beginning, though that was speedily overshadowed by the magnitude the matter had assumed as the volumes increased. I recognized that nothing I could ever accomplish in the way of publishing would warrant such an outlay as I was then making. It was not long before any idea I may have entertained in the way of pecuniary return was abandoned; there was no money in making the collection, or in any literary work connected with it. Yet certain books I knew to be intrinsically valuable. It was understood from the first that nothing in my collection was for sale; sometime, I thought, the whole might be sold to a library or public institution; but I would wait, at least, until the collection was complete.

I had now, perhaps, a thousand volumes, and began to be pretty well satisfied with my efforts. When, however, in 1862 I visited London and Paris, and rummaged the enormous stocks of second-hand books in the hundreds of stores of that class, my eyes began to open. I had much more yet to do. And so it was, when the collection had reached one thousand volumes, I fancied I had them all; when it had grown to five thousand, I saw it was but begun. As my time was short, I determined to make a thorough search all over Europe and complete my collection as soon as I could command the leisure.

This opportunity offered itself in 1866, when others felt competent to take charge of the business. On the 17th of August I landed with my wife at Queenstown, spent a week in Dublin, passed from the Giant's causeway to Belfast and Edinburgh, and after the tour of the lakes proceeded to London, the book mart of the world, where I might feed my desires to the full.

During all this time my mind had dwelt more and more upon the subject, and the vague ideas of materials for history which originally floated through my brain began to assume more definite proportions, though I had no thought, as yet, of ever attempting to write such a history myself. But I was obliged to think more or less on the subject in order to determine the limits of my collection. So far I had searched little for Mexican literature. Books on Lower California and northern Mexico I had bought, but Mexican history and archaeology proper had been passed over. Now the question arose, Where shall I draw the dividing line? Hence, to gather all the material requisite for a complete narrative of events bearing on California, it would be necessary to include a large part of the early history of Mexico, since the two were so blended as to make it impossible to separate them. It was my custom when collecting to glance through any book which I thought might contain information on the territory marked out. I did not stop to consider, I did not care, whether the book was of any value or not; it was easier and cheaper to buy it than to spend time in examining its value. Besides, in making such a collection it is impossible to determine at a glance what is of value and what is not. The most worthless trash may prove some fact wherein the best book is deficient, and this makes the trash valuable.

Gradually and almost imperceptibly had the area of my efforts enlarged. From Oregon it was but a step to British Columbia and Alaska; and as I was obliged for California to go to Mexico and Spain, it finally became settled in my mind to make the western half of North America my field, including in it the whole of Mexico and Central America. Thereupon I searched Europe for information concerning their New World relations.

In London I spent about three months, and went faithfully through every catalogue and every stock of books likely to contain anything on the Pacific coast. I employed a man to search the principal libraries, and make a transcript of the title of every book, manuscript, pamphlet, and magazine article, touching this territory, with brief notes on the subject-matter. The titles and abstracts were entered upon paper cards about four inches square. The cost of this catalogue was a little over a thousand dollars.[1]

From London I went to Paris, and searched the stalls, antiquarian warehouses, and catalogues, in the same careful manner. Leaving Paris the 3d of January, 1867, I went down into Spain. From there I travelled to Italy, Switzerland, Holland, Germany and Austria, and finally back to New York and Buffalo. Everywhere I found something, and seized upon it, however insignificant, for I had long since ceased to resist the malady. Often have I taken a cab or a carriage to drive me from stall to stall all day, without obtaining more than perhaps three or four books or pamphlets, for which I paid a shilling or a franc each. Then again I would light upon a valuable manuscript which relieved my pocket to the extent of three, five, or eight hundred dollars.

Now, I thought, my task is done. I have rifled America of its treasures; Europe have I ransacked; and after my success in Spain,

Asia and Africa may as well be passed by. I have ten thousand volumes and over, fifty times more than ever I dreamed were in existence when the collecting began. My library is a *fait accompli.* Here will I rest.

But softly! What is this inch-thick pamphlet that comes to me by mail from my agent in London? Stripping off the cover I read the title-page: *Catalogue de la Riche Bibliotèque de D. José María Andrade.* Seven thousand books direct from Mexico, and probably half of them works which should be added to my collection! What was to be done? Here were treasures beside which the gold, silver, and rich merchandise found by Ali Baba in the robbers' cave were dross. A new light broke in upon me. I had never considered that Mexico had been printing books for three and a quarter centuries—one hundred years longer than Massachusetts.

José María Andrade combined in himself the publisher, journalist, *littérateur*, bibliopole, and bibliophile; and the tenacity with which he clung to his collection was remarkable. It was ever the earnest desire of the unfortunate Maximilian to advance the interests of the country in every way; prominent among his many praiseworthy designs was that of improving the mental condition of the people by the elevation of literature. He began the formation of an imperial library, accomplished by enlisting the coöperation of Señor Andrade, the intelligent and zealous collector. It was arranged that, for a certain sum of money to be paid the owner of the books, this magnificent collection should form the basis of a *Biblioteca Imperial de Mejico.* But unfortunately for Mexico this was not to be. Evil befell both emperor and bibliophile. The former met the fate of many another adventurer of less noble birth and less chivalrous and pure intention, and the latter failed to secure his money.

When it became certain that Maximilian was doomed to die at the hands of his captors, Señor Andrade determined to secure to himself the proceeds from the sale of his library as best he might. Never since the burning of the Aztec manuscripts by the bigot Zumárraga had there fallen on the country such a loss.

Shutting my eyes to the consequences, therefore, I did the only thing possible under the circumstances to secure a portion of that collection: I telegraphed my agent in London five thousand dollars earnest money, with instructions to attend the sale and purchase at his discretion.

Thus it was that in 1869, ten years after beginning to collect, I found in my possession, including pamphlets, about sixteen thousand volumes; and with these, which even before its completion I placed on the fifth floor of the Market-street building, I concluded to begin work. As a collector, however, I continued lying in wait for opportunities.

VIII

THE LIBRARY

❧

My **library,** when first it came to be called a library, occupied one corner of the second story of the bookstore building on Merchant street, which connected with the front room on Montgomery street. When placed on the fifth floor of the Market-street building, it occupied room equivalent to thirty-five by one hundred and seventy feet, with a half mile and more of shelving against the walls. Following the works of reference, the books were arranged alphabetically by authors. On the east side were four rooms, two occupied as sleeping apartments by Mr Oak and Mr Nemos, and two used as working rooms by Mrs Victor and myself. There was one large draughtsman's working-counter, with drawers and a rack for maps. A large, high, revolving table occupied the centre of my room. Attached to it was a stationary stand into which it fitted, or rather of which it formed part. At this table I could stand, or by means of a high chair with revolving seat, I could sit at it and write on the stationary part. No place could better have suited my purpose but for interruptions, for I was never entirely free from business.

Yet, all through the dozen years the library was there, I trembled for its safety through fear of fire, as indeed did many others who appreciate its historical significance to this coast, well knowing that once lost, no power on earth could reproduce it. Hence its place in this building was regarded as temporary from the first.

Now and then the danger would be more vividly brought home to us by the alarm of fire on the premises; once in particular a fire broke out in the basement of the furniture store occupying the western side of the building, filling the library with dense smoke, and driving the inmates to the roof. The furniture store was nearly destroyed, and the bookstore suffered serious damage. It was a narrow escape for the library.

Thus, when in the autumn of 1881 Mr William B. Bancroft, my nephew, in charge of the manufacturing department, regarded the room as essential to his ever growing purposes, and as the money could be spared, I lent a willing ear.

First to be considered in choosing a new locality was whether the library should remain on the peninsula of San Francisco or take its place at some point across the bay. We finally concluded to remain in the city. In making such selection I could not take as fully into the account as I would have liked the influence of a library upon its locality. For example, who shall say what might or might not be the effects upon the graduating members of a great institution of learning, or upon the assembled law-makers for the nation, or upon that class of wealthy and intelligent inhabitants of the commercial metropolis who delight in scientific or historic association for the good of their country?

After some search, a place was found uniting several advantages and which on the whole proved satisfactory. It was on Valencia street, the natural continuation of Market street, on the line of the city's growth, and reached by the cars from the ferry which passed the store. There, on the west side, near its junction with Mission street, I purchased a lot one hundred and twenty by one hundred and twenty-six feet in size, and proceeded forthwith to erect a substantial two story and basement brick building, forty by sixty feet. In order that the building might be always detached it was placed in the centre of the lot, and to make it more secure from fire all the openings were covered with iron.

The Bancroft Library at 1538 Valencia Street, c. 1900,
courtesy of The Bancroft Library (1905.11574-FR)

A high fence was erected on two sides for protection against the
wind, and the grounds were filled with trees, grass, and flowers,
making the place a little Eden. On the glass over the entrance
was placed the number, 1538, and on the door a plate lettered in
plain script, THE BANCROFT LIBRARY.

The building proved most satisfactory. No attempt was made
at elaboration, either without or within; plain neat good taste,
with comfort and convenience, was alone aimed at. Every part of
it was ordered with an eye single to the purpose; the rooms are
spacious, there are plenty of large windows, and the building is
well ventilated. From the front door the main room, lower floor,
has wall shelves, holding for the most part sets and various collections aggregating 16,000 volumes. These sets are conveniently
lettered and numbered, in a manner that renders each work readily
accessible. They consist of large collections of voyages and travels;
of documents, periodicals, legislative and other public papers of

the federal government and the several states and territories of the Pacific slope; of laws, briefs, and legal reports; series of scrapbooks, almanacs, directories, bound collections of pamphlets, cumbersome folios, Mexican sermons, and other miscellaneous matter. Three lofty double tiers of shelving, extending across the room, are loaded with 500 bulky files of Pacific States newspapers, amounting to over 5000 volumes. It is a somewhat unwieldy mass, but indispensable to the local historian. Also was built and placed here a huge case, with drawers for maps, geographically arranged; also cases containing the card index, and paper bags of notes.

In the room above, the main library and working room, seated at tables, are a dozen literary workmen, each busy with his special task. The walls are filled with shelving nine tiers high, containing four classes of books. Most of the space is occupied by works of the first class, printed books, each volume bearing a number, and the numbers running consecutively from one to 12,000 under alphabetical arrangement, and afterward without arrangement, as additions are made indefinitely. The second class consists of rare books, of about 400 volumes, set apart by

Second Floor, Library Work Area of the Valencia Street Bancroft Library, engraving, c. 1881, courtesy of The Bancroft Library (1905.1168-FR)

reason of their great value, not merely pecuniary, though the volumes will bring from $35 to $800 each in the book markets of the world, but literary value, representing standard authorities, bibliographic curiosities, specimens of early printing and rare linguistics. The third class is composed entirely of manuscripts in 1200 volumes. The fourth class is made up of 450 works of reference and bibliographies. When the collection was placed in the library building it numbered 35,000 volumes, since which time additions have steadily been made, until the number now approaches 50,000. At the east end of the upper room is situated my private apartment, while at the other end are the rooms of Mrs Victor, Mr Nemos, and Mr Oak. All otherwise unoccupied wall space, above and below, is filled with portraits, plans, and other drawings, engravings, and unique specimens, all having reference to the territory covered by the collection.

Considerable inconvenience had been experienced during the first twelve years' use of the library, for want of proper numbering and cataloguing. For a time an alphabetical arrangement answered every purpose, but under this system books were so often out of place, and losses so frequent, that it was deemed best on removing to Valencia street to adopt a book-mark, a system of numbering, and make a new catalogue. The book-mark consisted of a lithographed line in plain script letters, The Bancroft Library, with the number. The catalogue indicates the shelf position of every book in the library; and the plan admits of additions almost limitless without breaking the alphabetic order.

In describing the contents of the library, aside from its arrangement in the building, one would classify it somewhat differently, territory and chronology taking precedence of outward form and convenience. We can merely glance at the several natural divisions of the subject, namely, aboriginal literature, sixteenth-century productions, works of the seventeenth and eighteenth centuries, nineteenth-century publications, maps, manuscripts, and the material for California and Northwest Coast history.

No one can know, not having had the experience, the endless labor and detail attending the keeping in order and under control of a large and rapidly growing collection of historical data.

A collection of books, like everything else, has its history and individuality. From the ordinary point of view there is nothing remarkable in gathering 50,000 volumes and providing a building for their reception. There are many libraries larger than this, some of them having been founded and carried forward by an individual. Nevertheless, there are some remarkable features about this collection.

Says an eminent writer: "Respecting Mr Bancroft's Pacific Library as a storehouse of historic data…but one opinion has been expressed during the twenty years that the existence of such an institution has been known to the world.…Disinterested and impartial visitors, after a personal inspection, have invariably shown a degree of admiration far exceeding that of the warmest friends who knew the library only from description.…There is no American collection with which this can fairly be compared.…" It is certain that at the present day no collection of books is worthy of the name of library without a fair share of these rare and valuable works, particularly works of material interest and value relating to the discovery, conquest, settlement, and development of America, in its many parts from south to north, and east to west, from the days of Columbus to the present time—books becoming every day rarer and more costly.

Thus in these various forms and attitudes the magnitude and importance of my work kept coming up and urging me on. This western coast, it seemed to me as I came to know and love it, is the best part of the United States, a nation occupying the best part of the two Americas, and rapidly becoming the most intellectual and powerful in the world. Its early history and all the data connected with it which can be gathered is of corresponding importance.

When the time comes, California and the commonwealths around, and up and down this Pacific seaboard, will be a seat of culture and power to which all roads shall lead.

IX

DESPERATE ATTEMPTS AT GREAT THINGS

≋

EAPS AND HEAPS of diamonds and—sawdust! Good
gold and genuine silver, pearls and oyster-shells, copper
and iron mixed with refuse and débris—such was the nature and
condition of my collection in 1869, before any considerable labor
had been bestowed upon it. Surrounded by these accumulations,
I sat in an embarrassment of wealth. Chaff and wheat; wheat,
straw, and dirt; where was the brain or the score of brains to do
this winnowing?

What winnowing? I never promised myself or anyone to
do more than to gather; never promised even that, and probably, had I known in the beginning what was before me, I never
should have undertaken it. Was it not enough to mine for the
precious metal without having to attempt the more delicate and
difficult task of melting down the mass and refining it, when I
knew nothing of such chemistry? But I could at least arrange my
accumulations in some kind of order, and even dignify them by
the name of library.

Meanwhile I had engaged as assistant, an Englishman of
erratic mind and manner, who called himself Bosquetti. Bosquetti
was directed to arrange and catalogue large additions lately made
to the library. He had been thus occupied about a month when
I engaged Mr Oak to assist him. Oak knew little of books except
such as he had studied at college, but he possessed to an eminent

Henry L. Oak, c. 1870,
courtesy of The Bancroft Library (Oak, Henry—POR1)

degree that rarest of qualities, common-sense. Within a few weeks
he had familiarized himself with the best systems, improving on
them all in many respects, or at least he had taken from them
such parts as best befitted his work and had applied them to it.
Thick medium writing paper was cut to a uniform size, three
and a half by five inches, and the full titles were written thereon;
these were then abridged on smaller cards, two and a half by four
inches, and finally copied alphabetically in a blank book made

for that purpose. Oak may be said to have done the whole of the cataloguing himself.

Oak was in sole charge of the literary accumulations, of which he was duly installed librarian. Oak continued copying into a book the contents of the small cards previously prepared, and thus made the first manuscript catalogue of the library, which was in daily use for a period of twelve years. He was assisted a portion of the time by a cousin of mine, son of my most esteemed friend and uncle, W. W. Bancroft, of Granville. During this time I made some passes at literature, writing for the most part at my residence. Shortly after we had fairly moved into the Market-street building, the full effects of the business depression before mentioned were upon us. The business outlook was not flattering, but nevertheless we pressed forward, well knowing that to falter was perdition.

During the autumn of 1870 Mr Oak continued his labors on the fifth floor, cataloguing new lots of books as they came in, arranging maps, briefs, and newspapers, copying and clipping bibliographical notes from catalogues, and taking care of the books and room. It was still my intention in due time to issue a bibliography of the Pacific coast, which should include all of my own collection and as many more titles as I could find. Before the end of the year there was quite a pile of my own manuscript on my table, and in the drawers, monographs, mostly, on subjects and incidents connected with the Pacific coast. All my thoughts were on history, and topics kindred thereto, Pacific States history, and the many quaint and curious things and remarkable and thrilling events connected therewith. I was passionately fond of writing; I would take up a subject here or an episode there and write it up for the pure pleasure it gave me, and every day I found myself able with greater ease and facility to discharge my thoughts on paper. But even yet I had no well defined intentions of writing a book for publication. The responsibility was greater than I cared to assume. I had seen in my business so many futile attempts in that direction, so many failures, that I had no desire to add mine to the number.

I continued writing, though in a somewhat desultory manner; the idea of anything more systematic at this time was somewhat repugnant to me. As yet my feebly kindled enthusiasm refused to burn brightly. I longed to do something, I did not know what; I longed to do great things, I did not know how; I longed to say something, I had nothing to say. And yet I would write as if my life depended on it. The difficulty, so far as more systemic effort was concerned, was to fell the incubi of care, and of pecuniary responsibility that leech-like had fastened themselves upon me these twenty years, and now threatened destruction to any plans I might make.

Long before I had a thought of writing anything myself for publication, the plan of an encyclopædia of the Pacific States had been proposed to me by several gentlemen of California who had felt the need of such a work. The idea presented itself thus: My collection, they said, was composed of every species of matter relating to the coast—physical geography, geology, botany, ethnology, history, biography, and so on through the whole range of knowledge. Was it not desirable to give to the world the fruits of such a field in the most compact shape, and was not an encyclopædia the natural, and indeed the only feasible form?

I did not at all fancy the task which they would thus lay upon me. It was not to my taste to manipulate knowledge merely. Yet it was true that an encyclopædia of knowledge relating wholly to the territory covered by the collection would certainly be desirable.

Ten days in the spring of 1871 were thus spent by Mr Oak in attending to the preparation of two guide-books for tourists, the publication of which I had undertaken, and in discussing the scheme of an encyclopædia, which I finally consented to superintend. I then began to look about for contributors. It was desirable at once to draw out as much as possible of talent latent on this coast, and at the same time to secure the best writers for the work. Circulars were accordingly issued, not only to men eminent in literature and the professions, but to pioneers, and to all likely to possess information, stating the purpose and requesting co-operation. To several of the judges, lawyers, physicians, clergymen, and others in San Francisco of known literary tastes and talents, I made personal appeals, and received flattering assurances.

FOR THE FIRST time in my life my health now began to fail. The increasing demands of the vast mercantile and manu-facturing structure which I had reared drew heavily upon my nervous system. I grew irritable, was at times despondent, and occasionally desperately indifferent. I determined on a change of scene. Accordingly, the 10th of May I started for the purpose of recreation and recuperation on a visit to the east, stopping at Salt Lake City for the purpose of enlisting the Mormons in my behalf. President Brigham Young[1] and the leading elders entered heartily into my project, and a scheme was devised for obtain-ing information from every part of Utah. With the intention of calling on my return, I continued my journey. Then I fell into despondency. The state of my nerves and the uncertainty of my financial future had so dissipated ambition that much of the time I found myself in a mood fitter for making my exit from the world than for beginning a new life in it.

At this time the chances that any important results would ever emanate from the library through my intervention were very slight. Gradually I abandoned the idea of having anything to do with any encyclopædia. My energies were sapped. I had helmed the ship of business until exhausted, and the storm continuing, I left it to others, little caring, so far as I was personally concerned, whether it weathered the gale or not. Such was my humor during

H. H. Bancroft, c. 1880s,
courtesy of The Bancroft Library (Bancroft, Hubert Howe—PORI)

the summer of 1871 as I lounged about among my friends at the east, listless and purposeless.

From this lethargy I was awakened by the accidental remark of a lady at whose house I was visiting with my daughter. She was an earnest, practical woman, cool and calculating, one whose friendship had been of long duration, and whose counsel now was as wise as it was beneficent. Clearly comprehending the situation, she saw that for me activity was life, passivity death, and her mind seemed to dwell on it. One day she said to me, "The next ten years will be the best of your life; what are you going to do with them?" A leading question, truly, and one I had often asked myself of late without ability to answer; yet her womanly way of putting these few simple words brought them home to me in a manner I had never before felt.

What was I to do? I did not know; but I would do something, and that at once. I would mark out a path and follow it, and if in the mean time I should be overwhelmed, let it be so; I would waste no more time waiting. Once more I rubbed my lamp and asked the genius what to do. In due time the answer came; the way was made clear, yet not all at once; still, from that time I was at less loss as to what next I should do and how I should proceed to do it. From that day to this I have known less wavering, less hesitation. I would make an effort, whatever the result, which should be ennobling, in which even failure should be infinitely better than listless inaction. Exactly what I would undertake I could not now determine. History-writing I conceived to be among the highest of human occupations, and this should be my choice, were my ability equal to my ambition. There was enough with which to wrestle, under these new conditions, to strengthen nerve and sharpen skill.

Thus roused I went back to California. I entered the library. Oak, alone and rudderless on a sudorific sea, was faithfully at work cutting up duplicate copies of books and severalizing the parts upon the previous plan, thus adding to the numerous scraps hitherto collected and arranged. It was a sorrowful attempt at great things; nevertheless it was an attempt. To this day the fruits of many such plantings in connection with these Literary Industries remain unplucked. Yet, if never permitted by my destiny to accomplish great things, I could at least die attempting them.

X

A LITERARY
WORKSHOP

❧

I T WAS THE 20th of August, 1871, that I returned from my eastern trip, being summoned to the support of a greatly imperiled business. My friends had become fearful for the safety of the firm, and had telegraphed me to return.

I was in a bad humor for business. I never thought it possible so to hate it, and all the belittlings and soul-crushings connected with it. "Only those who know the supremacy of the intellectual life," says George Eliot, "the life which has a seed of ennobling thought and purpose within it, can understand the grief of one who falls from that serene activity into the absorbing soul-wasting struggle with worldly annoyances." Had I been alone, with only myself to suffer, and had not even my literary aspirations been dependent on the success of the shop, I would have turned my back on it forever to let it sink or swim, as it pleased or was able.

This, however, was not to be. My duty was too plain before me. The business must have my attention; it must have more money, and I must provide it. Into the breach I threw myself, though at such a cost of feeling as no one ever knew, and as few could ever appreciate. Having done this, all that I could do to save the business, I mentally consigned the whole establishment to oblivion, and directed my attention once more, and this time in desperate earnest, to my literary infatuation.

At the very threshold of my resolve, however, stared me in the face the old inquiry, What shall I do, and how shall I do it? One thing was plain, even to a mind as unskilled in the mysteries of book-making as mine. On my shelves were tons of unwinnowed material for histories unwritten and sciences undeveloped. To find a way to the gold of this amalgam, to mark out a path through a wilderness of knowledge to the desired facts, was the first thing to be done. He who would write at the greatest advantage on any practical subject must have before him all that has been written by others, all knowledge extant on that subject. To have that knowledge upon his shelves, and yet be unable to place his hand upon it, is no better than to be without it. If I wished to write fully on the zoology, for example, of the Pacific slope, nine tenths of all the books in my library containing reference to the animals of the coast might as well be at the bottom of the ocean as in my possession unless I was prepared to spend fifteen years on this one subject. And even then it could not be thoroughly done.

Thus before authorship could begin, a magic wand must be waved over the assembled products of ten thousand minds, which would severalize what each had said on all important topics, and reduce the otherwise rebellious mass to form and system.

How was this to be accomplished? It is at the initial period of an undertaking that the chief difficulty arises. I had no guide, no precedent by which to formulate my operations. To my knowledge, authorship of the quality to which I aspired had never before been attempted by a private individual. The great trouble was to get at and abstract the information. Toward the accomplishment of this my first efforts were crude, as may well be imagined. I attempted to read or cursorily examine such volumes as were likely to contain information on the subjects to be written, and to mark the passages to be extracted. A system of figures was adopted, one of which, pencilled on the margin of the page, denoted the subject-heading under which the extracted page or paragraph should appear. These passages were then copied.

After going over a dozen volumes or so in this manner, and estimating the time required for reading and marking all the books of the library, I found that by constant application, eight hours a day, it would take four hundred years to go through the books of the library in a superficial way. I concluded, therefore, that other men must also be set to read, and more men to copy literatim all information to be required in the study of any subject. Thus these literary industries began gradually to assume broader proportions, and so they continued till December of this same year.

On trial, however, the plan proved a failure. On beginning to write, I found the extracts unsatisfying and felt the necessity of the book itself. The copyist may have made a mistake; and to appraise the passage at its full value I must see the connection. Any experienced author could have told me this; but there was no experienced author at hand.

After some twenty-five reams of legal paper had thus been covered on one side, to consign the labors of these six or eight men for these several months to the waste heap was but the work of a moment. There was too much involved, the enterprise was projected on too large a scale, to admit of a wrong beginning; it appeared folly to continue a path shown to be wrong.

Meanwhile, after frequent and protracted discussions, I determined to have the whole library indexed as one would index a single book.

Among other parts of the outlined encyclopædia was a collection of voyages and travels to and throughout the Pacific States. As the more comprehensive programme was gradually set aside, my attention became more and more concentrated on these several parts. True history was ever the prominent idea in

my mind, but, audacious as was my ambition, I had not the pre-
sumption to rush headlong into it during the incipient stages of
my work. At the beginning of my literary pilgrimage, I did little
but flounder in a slough of despond. Until my feet touched more
solid ground, I did not dare essay that which appeared to me no
less difficult than grand.

During the first half of 1872, in conjunction with the indexing,
under a devised system of condensation, several persons were
employed in extracting Pacific coast voyages and travels. Mr Ora
Oak, a younger brother of the librarian, was so employed for some
time. Walter M. Fisher wrote out the travels of Bryant, Taylor,
Humboldt, and others.

Several women were also employed upon these voyages. I
know not why it is, but almost every attempt to employ female
talent in connection with these Industries has proved a signal
failure. I have to-day nothing to show for thousands of dollars
paid out for the futile attempts of female writers. What it is they
lack, justly attributable to their sex, I hardly know. That a woman
has not the mental or physical force and endurance of a man does
not seem a sufficient reason. True, in literary labors, strength is
taxed to the utmost. I have tried many occupations, and there
is no kind of work, I venture to say, so wearing as literary labor. If
a woman has genius, that is another thing. But even then genius
alone is of little avail to me. My work demands drudgery as well. If
she have genius, let her stay at home, write from her effervescent
brain, and sell the product to the highest bidder.

Hard work, the hardest of work, is not for frail and tender
woman. It were a sin to place it on her. Give her a home, with bread
and babies; love her, treat her kindly, give her all the rights she
desires, even the defiling right of suffrage if she can enjoy it, and
she will be your sweetest, loveliest, purest, and most devoted companion. But life-long application, involving life-long self-denial,

involving constant pressure on the brain, constant tension of the sinews, is not for women, but for male philosophers or—fools. So, long since, I forswore petticoats in my library; breeches are sometimes bad enough, but when unbefitting they are disposed of somewhat more easily.

Later in my work, and as an exception to the above, I am glad to testify to the ability and success of one female writer, if for no other reason than to deliver me from the charge of prejudice. I have found in Mrs Frances Fuller Victor, during her arduous labors for a period of ten years in my library, a lady of cultivated mind, of ability and singular application; likewise her physical endurance was remarkable.

Long before this I had discovered the plan of the index then in progress to be impracticable. Others realized this more fully than myself, and from them came many suggestions in perfecting the present and more practical system. Three months were occupied in planning and testing this new system. Mr William Nemos came in, and as he quickly mastered the system and displayed marked ability in various directions, the indexing and the indexers were placed under his supervision.

Thus book by book of the authorities collected was passed through the hands of skilled assistants, and with checks and counter-checks an immense and all-comprehending system of indexing was applied to each volume. Physical, moral, geographical, historical, from the fibre of an Eskimo's hair to the *coup de maître* of Cortés, nothing was too insignificant or too great to find its place there.

One would think it easy to find men who could make this index. But it was not so. The difficulty was this: to be of value, the work must all be done on a uniform plan. One person could not do all; from five to twenty men were constantly employed upon it for years.

Finally the cards were all classified under their distinguishing title, and placed in alphabetical order in upright cupboard-like cases made for the purpose. Such was the machinery which we found necessary to contrive in order to extract the desired material from the cumbersome mass before us.

XI

SOME OF MY ASSISTANTS

≈

THOSE TO WHOM I apply the term assistants by no means include all the army of workers who have at various times and in various ways lent me their services in my historical efforts. During the long term of my labors, it is safe to say that no less than six hundred different persons were at work for me at various times in my library. At the minimum, the number engaged in the library at any one time during a period of thirty years seldom fell below twelve; the highest being fifty, some thirty of whom were on regular details. My assistants proper are those who aided me in my more responsible labors, and may be reduced to twenty in all, though more than a hundred made the effort unsuccessfully at one time or another.

All my life, whatever I have had in hand, whether in the field of business or of literature, I have always been fortunate enough to have good men about me, not only efficient aids, but those whom I could call my friends, and the enjoyment of whose regard was ever a source of gratification. While the responsibility must always rest upon me alone, some portion of that praise which has been so lavishly bestowed upon me and my enterprise rightly belongs to them.

Here I provide information about a few of these able assistants.

First among my collaborators I may mention here Henry Lebbeus Oak. I have often regarded it as remarkable that so true and conscientious a friend, so faithful a librarian and laborer, should so early and opportunely have come to my aid. He was born at Garland, Maine, on the 13th of May, 1844. Raised in New Hampshire, he attended Bowdoin College, and for a while taught school, while contemplating studies in law or book-keeping. California then came to his rescue, as she has rescued many another, saving some from hell, but vastly more from heaven. He came on a steamer in 1866 and ended up becoming a principal of a Hayward public school through John Swett[1] in the spring of 1867, followed by a term at a Methodist institute in Napa. After coming to San Francisco, he served as a teacher again for a period, then was employed as office editor of the *Occident* newspaper. A year later, when the publication of that paper passed from the control of our firm, he assumed the position of librarian and superintendent of that wide range of intricate detail essential to extracting material in the Bancroft library, a place he held continuously for a period of nearly twenty years. I suppose nature has a place and purpose for everything she makes, though it would seem that not everything made by nature finds its place and purpose. This man, however, certainly found his vocation, and fitted himself to it perfectly.

Never was there a more devoted, faithful worker in any field than my valued friend William Nemos, a nom de plume by which he preferred to be known among us. Born in February 1848 in Finland, Nemos attended high school in Stockholm to prepare for Upsala university, but family matters compelled him to go to London and enter business. He favored studies in philosophy. He left Liverpool in the spring of 1870 for Australia, and ended up in the mines in vain, his money stolen. Nemos then proceeded to California via Hawaii, arriving in midsummer 1871. After a stint in Oregon, he returned to San Francisco in 1873 and obtained work in the library.

Thomas Savage was born in Habana, of New England parents, the 27th of August, 1823. When nine years of age the boy could speak Spanish better than English or French. He read the Latin classics and prepared himself for the legal profession. His father died when Thomas was quite young. Ill health obliged him to abandon study. Many times his life was despaired of, and ever since I have known him he has been a constant sufferer; yet all the while he has worked as industriously and as cheerfully as if enjoying the best health. Several children were the result of marriage, but within a period of ten years Mr Savage buried thirteen members of his family. A few years as book-keeper were followed by an engagement in the United States consulate at Habana, for twenty-one and a half years. Thus it was that his thorough knowledge of the Spanish language, and his long experience in consular business, rendered invaluable his services in the library. In 1867 Mr Savage retired from the consulate at Habana, then went to San Salvador, where he was appointed United States consul. He continued on to Guatemala. The 26th of March, 1873, he arrived at San Francisco, and four months afterward entered the library. For many years Mr Savage was my main reliance on Spanish-American affairs. All my chief assistants were good Spanish scholars, but all in cases of doubt were glad to refer to him as an expert.

Frances Fuller was born in Rome, New York, May 23, 1826, and was educated at the seminary in Ohio, whither her parents removed. Starting at the age of fourteen she contributed to the county papers. When her father died, there was real work to do. Her sister Metta was also a successful writer, but Frances possessed a wider range of intellectual powers. The two sisters, twin souls, married two brothers. Frances married Henry C. Victor, a naval engineer, and accompanied him first to San Francisco and then to Oregon. Her letters in the *Bulletin*, articles in the *Overland Monthly*, and her books show how cordially she entered into the exploration of a fresh field. In 1878 she accepted a hint from me, and came readily to my assistance, with greater enthusiasm than one less acquainted with her subject could be expected to feel. In ability, conscientiousness, and never-ceasing interest and faithfulness Mrs Victor was surpassed by none.

There were many of Spanish and Mexican origin. Month after month they plodded more or less diligently along, as part of the great combination. Of these, Vicente P. Gomez was one. A native of Mexico, he came to California when a child. He wrote a beautiful hand, and spoke the most graceful Spanish of any man in California. He was the Victor of Bret Harte's *Story of a Mine*. Besides laboring long and faithfully at the surveyor's office extracting material from the archives, he accompanied Mr Savage on the same mission. But far more important than all this was the manuscript volume of 430 pages of his own reminiscences. While extracting material for history, or in conversation, wherever he happened to be, we had a man ready to take them down. The result was a most magnificent contribution to the historical literature of the west.[2]

XII

MY FIRST BOOK

T URNING-POINTS IN LIFE are not always mere accident. Often they are the result of teachings or inborn aspirations, and always they are fraught with some moral lesson of special significance.

From the depths of despair I would sometimes rise to the firm conviction that with my facilities and determined purpose I could not only do this work, but that I could save to these Pacific States more of their early incidents than had been preserved to other nations; that I could place on record annals exceptionally complete and truthful; that I could write a history which as a piece of thorough work, if unaccompanied by any other excellence, would be given a place among the histories of the world.

If ever fancy whispered I could write well, I had but to read a page of Shakespeare, whose every finished sentence is a string of pearls, and the fountain of my ambition would dwindle to insignificance. What were my miserable efforts beside the conceptions of a Dante? However, become possessed with an idea, and you will then find language according to your ability to express it; it is poverty of ideas that makes men complain of the poverty of language.

Thus the billows of despondency passed over me. Overwhelmed by the magnitude of my task, I sat for days and brooded, heart-sick and discouraged. What profiteth me this heavy labor? My mind is vapid, my nerves unstrung; I have not the strength, physical or intellectual, for work of such magnitude. I may succeed or I may fail. In either case some will approve, others will ridicule. And what is approval or ridicule to me? I do this work to please neither God nor man, but only myself. It is based on a selfishness almost as broad as that of patriots and propagandists. I must toil on, denying myself companionship, which indeed was small hardship; I must deprive myself of every pleasure, even of the blessed air and sunshine, the sweetest gifts of nature. These and nine tenths of the joys of association and recreation I must yield to musty books and dusty garret. All the powers of mind and body must be made captive to this one purpose.

There is a quality of intellectual application that will never be satisfied with less than grand results. And amidst such labors many cares are dissipated. As the Chinese say, "The dog in his kennel barks at his fleas, but the dog that is hunting does not feel them." Labor pursued as pleasure is light, yet he who seeks only pleasure in his work will never find it. Pleasure is a good chance acquaintance, but a bad companion. To read for my own pleasure or benefit was not sufficient for me; it was not consistent with the aims and industries of my past life, which were never content unless there appeared something tangible as the result of each year's endeavor. It is the useful, the beneficial alone which gives true enjoyment, and in the attainment of this there is often much pain. Yet if life like the olive is a bitter fruit, when pressed it yields sweet oil, Jean Paul Richter[1] would say.

Before my cooler judgment my self-imposed task presented itself in this form: Next after gathering, already partially accomplished, was the acquisition of power over the mass. From being slave of all this knowledge, I must become master. My object seemed to be the pride and satisfaction it would afford me to improve somewhat the records of my race, save something of a nation's history, which but for me would drop into oblivion; to catch from the mouths of living witnesses, just ready to take their final departure, important facts explaining new incidents and strange experiences; to originate and perfect a system by which means alone this history could be gathered and written; to lay the corner-stone of this fair land's literature while the land was yet young and ambitious.

Early in my efforts the conquest of Mexico attracted my attention. This story of the conquest possessed me with a thrilling interest; and before me lay the original authorities. These might be the guide of the literary fledgling. Ah! there was the trouble. Had the work not been done better than I could hope to do it? This mountain of my ambition after hard labor brought forth a few chapters of sententious nothings, and I cleared my table of authorities on the grand conquest.

At this time I was almost wholly occupied in handling the ideas of others; but it was not long before I began to have ideas of my own. It has always been my custom to examine carefully authorities currently held of little or no value. Not that I ever derived, or expected to derive, much benefit from them, but it was a satisfaction to know everything that had been written on the subject I was treating. And as for bias, though not pretending to be free from it—who that lives is?—yet were I ever knowingly to reach the point where pride of opinion was preferred before truth, I should wish from that moment to lay down my pen.

The introduction to my history was exclusively my own theme; in some subjects others might to some extent participate with me, but not in this. Hence, during the fourteen weeks that my really talented and intelligent assistant was floundering in a sea of erudition, with little or nothing available in the end to show for it, I myself had taken out material from which I easily wrote three hundred pages, though after twice re-arranging and rewriting I reduced it one half, eliminated half of what was left, and printed the remainder.

To form a critical estimate of our own literary ability is impossible. In all this the failure of certain of my assistants to prove profitable to my work was a source of small anxiety to me as compared with my own failures. If by securing help I might accomplish more, well; but the work itself must be mine alone, planned by me and executed by me.

And now was fully begun this new life of mine, the old life being dead. This change of life was as the birth of a new creature, a baptism in a new atmosphere. Looking back over the past my life lies spread before me in a series of lives, a succession of deaths and new life, until I feel myself older than time, though young and hopeful in my latest, newest life. I had now become fully imbued with the idea that there was a work to do, and that this was my work. I entered upon it with relish, and as I progressed, it satisfied me.

Following a fit of despondency, a triumph was like the dancing of light on the icy foliage after a gloomy storm. In planting and executing, in loading my mind and discharging it on paper, in finding outlet and expression to pent thought, in the healthful exercise of my mental faculties, I found relief such as I had never before experienced, relief from the corroding melancholy of stifled aspirations, and a pleasure more exquisite than any I had hitherto dreamed of.

ALTHOUGH MY *Native Races* cannot be called a chance creation, its coming as my first work in 1874 was purely accident. Following my general plan, which was a series of works on the western half of North America, and near the beginning of the whole project I became satisfied that I must of necessity treat of the aborigines. Wherever I touched the continent with my Spaniards they were there, a dusky, disgusting subject. I did not fancy them. I would gladly have avoided them. I was no archæologist, ethnologist, or antiquary, and had no desire to become such. My tastes in the matter, however, did not dispose of the subject. The savages were there, and there was no help for me; I must write them up to get rid of them.

It would not do to break off a narrative of events in order to describe the manners and customs, or the language or the mythology of a native nation. The reader should know something of both peoples thus introduced to each other before passing the introduction; he should know all about them.

Once settled that the natives must be described in a work set apart for them, the question arose, How should they be treated? Little else than raids, fightings, and exterminations we heard concerning them; these, coupled with opprobrious epithets which classed them as cattle rather than as human beings, tended in no wise to render the subject fascinating to me. Indeed I never could bring my pen to write the words 'buck,' 'squaw,' or 'Digger,' if I could help it. The first two are vulgarisms of the lowest order; the third belongs to no race or nation in particular, but was applied indiscriminately to the more debased natives of California and Nevada. They should be described as they stood in all their native glory, and before the withering hand of civilization was laid upon them.

Spreading before me the subject with hardly any other guide than practical common-sense, I resolved the question into its several divisions. What is it we wish to know about these people? I asked myself. In all my work I was determined to keep upon firm ground, to avoid meaningless and even technical terms, to avoid theories, speculations, and superstitions of every kind, and to deal only in facts. This I relied on more than on any other. Yet many things which were long since supposed to be settled were not settled, and much which I would be expected to decide never could be decided by any one.

Finally, after much deliberation to enable me to grasp the subject which lay spread over such a vast territory, I concluded to divide manners and customs into two parts, making of the wild or savage tribes one division, and of the civilized nations another. Indeed, like most of these expressions, the terms savage and civilized are purely relative. Where is the absolute savage on the face of the earth to-day; where the man absolutely perfect in his civilization? What we call civilization is not a fixed state, but an irresistible and eternal moving onward.

It was my purpose to lay before the world absolutely all that was known of these peoples at the time of the appearing among them of their European exterminators. The myths of these peoples, their strange conceptions of their origin, their deities, and their future state, would present a much more perfect and striking picture placed together where they might the better be analyzed and compared.

When my first division was wholly written I submitted it in turn to each of my principal assistants, and invited their criticism, assuring them that I should be best pleased with him who could find most fault with it. A number of suggestions were made, some of which I acted on. During the progress of this work I succeeded in utilizing the labors of my assistants to the full extent of my anticipations; indeed, it was necessary I should do so. Otherwise from a quarter to a half century would have been occupied in this one work. Fifty years! I had not so many to spare upon this work. The work of my assistants, besides saving me an immense amount of drudgery and manual labor, left my mind always fresh, and open to receive and retain the subject as a whole. I could institute comparisons and indulge in generalizations more freely, and I believe more effectually, than with my mind overwhelmed by a mass of detail. I do not know how far others have carried this system. Professors in the German universities are most prolific authors, and these almost to a man have the assistance of one or two students.

Thus says Hurst: "While the real author is responsible for every word that goes out under his own name, and can justly claim the parentage of the whole idea, plan, and scope of the work, he is spared much of the drudgery incident to all book-making which is not the immediate fruit of imagination. Where history is to be ransacked, facts to be grouped, and matters of pure detail to be gleaned from various sources, often another could do better service than the author." And the system is growing in favor in the United States.

XIII

THE PERILS OF
PUBLISHING

NOW I HAD to undergo the trials of publishing. Business experience had taught me that the immediate recognition, even of a work of merit, depends almost as much on the manner of bringing it forth as upon authorship.

Would the average newspaper publisher on the Pacific coast regard with the same eyes a book thrust suddenly and unheralded upon his attention as the production of a person whom he had never known except as a shopkeeper, one whom he had never suspected of aspiring to literature, as if the same book were placed before him with explanation, and bearing upon it the approving stamp of those whose opinions must overrule even his own? Hordes of literary adventurers are constantly coming and going, not one in a thousand of whom will be known a century hence. No book can live for fifty years unless it has merit; and no meritorious book in these present days can remain very long hidden.

Experience had told me that a book written, printed, and published at this date on the Pacific coast, no matter how meritorious or by whom sent forth, that is to say if done by any one worth the castigating, would surely be condemned by some and praised coldly and critically by others. Trade engenders competition, and competition creates enemies. There were hundreds in California who damned me every day, and to please this class as well as themselves there were newspaper writers who would like nothing better than, by sneers and innuendoes, to consign the fruits of laborious years to oblivion.

"This man is getting above his business," some would say. "Because he can sell books, he seems to infer a divine mission to write them. Now it may be well for him to understand that merchandising and authorship are two distinct things; that a commercial man who has dealt in books as he would deal in bricks, by count, weight, or dollars' worth, cannot suddenly assume to know all things and set himself up as a teacher of mankind. He must be put down. Such arrogance cannot be countenanced. If writing is thus made common, our occupation is gone."

All did not so feel; but there was more of such sentiment behind editorial spectacles than editors would admit even to themselves. I have seen through jealousy or conscienceless meanness the fruits of a good man's best days thrown to the dogs by some flippant remark of an unprincipled critic. Tuthill's *History of California*[1] was a good book, the best by far which up to its time had been written on the subject. And yet there were those among his brother editors in California who did not scruple to color their criticism from some insignificant flaws which they pretended to have discovered, and so consign a faithful, true history of this coast to perdition because the author had taken a step or two above them.

To local fame or a literary reputation restricted to California, I did not attach much value. Not that I was indifferent to the opinions of my neighbors, or that I distrust Pacific-coast journalists as a class. I had among them many warm friends whose approbation I coveted. But at this juncture I did not desire the criticism either of enemies or friends, but of strangers; I was desirous above all that my book should be first reviewed on its merits and by disinterested and unprejudiced men.

The reason is obvious. I dealt in facts, gathering from new fields and conveniently arranged. These were the raw material for students in the several branches of science, and for philosophers in their generalizations. This was their work; they would theorize, and generalize, and deduce for themselves. But they would not despise my facts. Hence it was by the verdict of the best men of the United States, of England, France, and Germany, the world's ripest scholars and deepest thinkers, that my contributions to knowledge must stay or fall.

To reach these results involved a journey to the eastern states. Yet before leaving this coast on such a mission there should be some recognition of my efforts here. It were not best for me to leave my state entirely unheralded.

Up to this time, about the beginning of 1874, I had spoken little of my work to any one, preferring to accomplish something first and then point to what I had done rather than talk about what I intended to do. I was fully aware that often the reputation which precedes performance is greater than that which comes after it, hence I would husband whatever good was to be said of me until it had something to rest on. During the previous year several notices had crept into the papers, mostly through visitors from the east, concerning the library and the work going on there. Members of the San Francisco press often came to me for information, but were asked to wait till I was ready to publish something on the subject. At present all I desired was to be let alone.

When the plan of the *Native Races* was fully settled, and the first volume, and parts of the second and third volumes were in type, I invited a number of men eminent in their several callings to inspect my work and report. The opinions formed from these investigations were forwarded to me in the form of letters, which I printed as a circular.

Some of these men were exceedingly interested and astonished. There was Professor George Davidson, for many years at the head of the United States coast survey, president of the academy of sciences. I sent my assistant Goldschmidt to him with a copy of the *Native Races* for his examination. Presently his attendant came to the door and addressed him while he was reading, reporting that several men were waiting to speak to the professor, to which Davidson exclaimed, "Let them wait! Such work as this doesn't fall into my hands every day."

The name I should give to the territory marked out had often troubled me. The Pacific States of North America, therefore, as the best and most fitting term for the designation of this territory, its past, present, and future, I finally settled upon.

At last I was ready for the newspaper reporters, if not for the reviewers. The *Bulletin, Alta, Post,* and *Chronicle* came out in long articles, vying with each other in the extent of their description and loudness of their praise.

I MUST PRESENTLY GO east, call upon fifty or a hundred of the leading literary men, scientists, and journalists, and explain personally to them the character of the work I was engaged in. This I dreaded. Proud and sensitive, I felt it to be a most difficult, most unpleasant task, one repugnant to my nature, which coveted retirement above all things else. Writers are sensitive. It is well they are. The thoroughbred is thinner-skinned than the ass. A man who is not sensitive about his reputation never will make one. I did not feel sure that my work was sufficiently meritorious to awaken their interest, that I had done anything to be proud of, and I did not know whether or not they would be interested. It came up to me as a series of beggary in which to indulge was worse than starvation.

Yet it must be done. I felt that I owed it to myself and to my work. Life and fortune were now fully embarked in this enterprise, and my enthusiasm for the work was mounting higher as the months and years went by. My first work was ready for publication, and on its reception would depend in a measure my whole future. I required the opinion of these men concerning it. No amount of writing would lay the matter before them as I could do myself. I must have direct and immediate assurance as to the quality of my work from the only class of men the critics feared, and then I should not fear the critics.

It was altogether a secondary matter whether copies of the book were sold or not. I merely wished to assure myself whether mine was a good work well performed, or a useless one poorly done. I would have the book issued by first-class publishers in New York and Europe, for it must bear upon it the stamp of a first-class publication, but the people might buy it or not as they pleased. It was no part of my purpose to publish my first work in San Francisco, or to permit the imprint of our firm upon the title-page. It seemed to me in bad taste for the author's name and publishing house to appear upon the same title page. Now I must obtain for it all the weight of a first-class eastern publisher, and not impart to it the appearance of having been originated by a bookseller as a commercial speculation. I had printed one hundred copies for private distribution.

Returned from my eastern pilgrimage, armed with letters from the high-priests of New England learning, I was ready to have my book reviewed in the *Overland Monthly*, the first and only literary journal of any pretensions west of the Rocky mountains. The editors suggested Mr Daniel C. Gilman,[2] president of the university of California; he had been a guest at my house, had frequently visited the library, spending considerable time there, and had always expressed much interest in my work. It was a favorite project of his in some way to transfer my library to the lands of the university, evidently with the idea that once there it would never be removed.

One day he came to me and stated that a building fund was about to be appropriated to the purpose of the university, that the plans of new buildings were drawn, and that if I would agree to move my library to Berkeley, without any other obligation expressed or implied, with full liberty at any time to remove it, he would have a building erected specially for the collection, and thereby lessen the danger to which it was then exposed of being destroyed by fire, for that would be a national calamity.

I declined. For, however free I might be to remove my collection, there would ever be resting over me an implied obligation which I was by no means willing to incur.

I felt the risk of fire, felt it every day. But I explained to the president that the library was not merely a reference library, but a working library; that I had imposed upon myself certain tasks which would occupy the better part of my life, if not, indeed, the whole of it, and it was more convenient both for me and for my assistants where it was. I must decline hampering my work in any way. Writing history of all things demands freedom; I was free, absolutely free. I sought neither emolument nor office from any quarter.

As for the article I hoped from Mr Gilman, his manuscript did not suit; it lacked bones, or any substantial framework. I felt very grateful to Mr Gilman for his kindness to me on many occasions. But here the life issue of my literary labors was at stake. I tore the manuscript in pieces.

Finally, Harcourt on my staff pursued Ross Browne of the *Overland*, and from Mr Browne I received a review that amounted to one of the best articles ever written upon the subject, in the *Overland* of December.

Then I went alike to my friends and my enemies of the San Francisco daily press. I placed in their hands my book; told them I was ready to have it reviewed. All were gracious. It was an enterprise of which they felt proud, and they heartily wished it every success.

Publishing having been my business, and the *Native Races* being my first book, persons have asked me if it paid pecuniarily; and when I answered No, they seemed at a loss what to make of it. Samuel Johnson says, "no man but a blockhead ever wrote except for money." I will admit myself a blockhead.

XIV

A LITERARY PILGRIM

≫

I SET OUT ON my pilgrimage the 3d of August, 1874, taking
with me my daughter Kate, to place in school at Farmington,
Connecticut. After a few days' stay at Buffalo with my two sisters,
Mrs Palmer and Mrs Trevett, I proceeded to New York.

In meetings to gain reviewers and a publisher, I went to
Hartford and to New Haven. In Hartford, President Gilman
introduced me to Professor Brewer of Yale, Doctor Asa Gray
of Harvard, and others. He also spoke of me to others, among
them Mr Warner of the *Courant*, who, when I called upon him
subsequently, greeted me with a scarcely anticipated kindness. I
was then in a humor to be won for life by any man who would
take the trouble. It may seem weak, this super-sensitiveness, but
I was in a feverish state of mind, and my nerves were all unstrung
by long labor. I was callous enough to ignorance and indifference,
for amongst these I had all along been working, but intelligent
sympathy touched me.

While attending the meetings of a scientific association my
attention was called to one Porter C. Bliss, whose name was on
the programme for several papers on Mexico. Mr Gilman, also
at this meeting, said I should know him and introduced me. He
was a singular character both without and within. His clothes
were neither neat nor well-fitting, leaving the appearance of the

Wandering Jew overtaken by Mexican highwaymen and forced to a partial exchange of apparel with them. His mind was no less disjointed than his manner. His was a disinterested devotion to other men's madness such as is seldom seen. Bliss revealed that he had some three thousand volumes he had collected in Mexico, stored in New York, and stated that I might accompany him thither to select at pleasure. In return I invited him to accompany me to Boston in this mission of mine, to which he assented with pleasure. Ultimately, he provided an addition to the library of some four or five hundred volumes.

Though this literary pilgrim from the unlettered west at first sought in vain sympathy and catholicity of sentiment among the scholars of New England, Bliss and I were destined in due time to come upon men with hearts as well as heads; and first among these was Doctor Asa Gray. He in turn gave me letters to Francis Parkman,[1] Charles Francis Adams,[2] and others.

James Russell Lowell[3] lived in a pleasant, plain house, common to the intellectual and refined of that locality. Lowell listened without saying a word. When I had finished, he entered warmly into the merits of the case, made several suggestions and discussed points of difference. He bound me to him forever by his many acts of sympathy then and afterward, for he never seemed to lose interest in my labors, and wrote me regarding them. "You have handled a complex, sometimes even tangled and tautological subject, with so much clearness and discrimination as to render it not merely useful to the man of science, but attractive to the general reader. The conscientious labor in collecting, and the skill shown in the convenient arrangement of such a vast body of material, deserve the highest praise."

On the 26th of August, after calling on several journalists in Boston, and an attempt to visit Mr Longfellow[4] in Nahant, we visited Wendell Phillips,[5] who gave me a welcome that did my heart good. Later upon receipt of the third volume he wrote me: "I read each chapter with growing interest. What a storehouse you provide for every form and department of history in time to come."

John G. Whittier[6] was a warm personal friend of Phillips. We went to Amesbury, where the poet resided. He gave me letters to Longfellow, Emerson,[7] and Doctor Barnard.[8] "I have been so much interested in his vast and splendid plan of a history of the western slope of our continent," he writes to Mr Longfellow, "that I take pleasure in giving him a note to thee. What material for poems will be gathered up in his volumes! It seems to me one of the noblest literary enterprises of our day."

I did not see Mr Longfellow, but he wrote me very cordially, praising my book and regretting he should have missed my call.

I hoped to get Francis Parkman to review my book in the *North American Review*, so to Parkman I went. "This shows wonderful research, and I think your arrangement is good, but I should have to review it upon its merits," said Mr Parkman.

"As a matter of course," I replied. And so the matter was left; and in due time several splendid reviews appeared in this important journal as the different volumes were published.

Returning to Boston, we took the train for Concord and sought Mr Emerson. He was gracious enough, and gave me some letters, but in all his doings the great philosopher was cold and unsympathetic. From Concord we went again to Cambridge, to see Mr Howells[9] of the *Atlantic Monthly*. It was finally arranged that Bliss was to write an article of some ten pages on my work for this magazine.

There were many others we called on, some absent, among them Oliver Wendell Holmes.[10] From Doctor Holmes I subsequently received many letters, which brought with them a world of refreshing encouragement. So genial and hearty were his expressions of praise that the manner of bestowal doubled its value to me. Of the third volume he wrote: "Your labor is, I believe, fully appreciated by the best judges; and you have done, and are doing a work for which posterity will thank you."

None were kinder than T. W. Higginson,[11] who was most kind in his review of the *Native Races* in *Scribner's Monthly* magazine. "That California was to be counted upon to yield wit and poetry was known by all; but the deliberate result of scholarly labor was just the product not reasonably to be expected from a community thirty years old. That kind of toil seemed to belong rather to a society a little maturer, to a region of public libraries and universities."

It was no great achievement to visit these men and command their attention.[12] And yet in the state of mind in which I was then laboring, it was one of the most disagreeable tasks of my life, and strong as I usually was physically, it sent me to bed and kept me there for a fortnight.

I had been entirely successful; but success here was won not as in San Francisco, by years of tender devotion to an ennobling cause, but by what I could not but feel to be an humiliating course. I sought men whom I did not wish to see, and talked with them of things about which of all others it was most distasteful to me to converse. It was false pride, however, and my extreme sensitiveness that kept alive these feelings. Good men assured me that I was not overstepping the bounds of literary decorum in thus thrusting my work forward upon the notice of the world; that my position was peculiar, and that in justice to my undertaking in San Francisco I could not do otherwise.

In New York I met George Bancroft—with whom, by the way, I am in no way related[13]—who gave me a letter to Doctor Draper,[14] and was kind enough afterward to write:

"To me you render an inestimable benefit; for you bring within reach the information which is scattered in thousands of volumes....Press on, my dear sir, in your great enterprise,...so that you may enjoy your well earned honors during what I hope may be a long series of later years."

It is perhaps one of the severest trials of an author's life, the first coming in contact with a publisher. It certainly would have been so with me in this instance, had I felt dependent on any of them. But as I proposed printing the work myself I had no fear regarding a publisher.

I was resolved that nothing within my power to remove should stand in the way of a complete success. Again and again have I plunged recklessly forward in my undertakings regardless of consequences, and but for the habit of thoroughness, might as well never have been done, with a dogged determination to spend as long as time or money lasted.

Of Mark Twain[15] and the *Native Races* says Charles Dudley Warner,[16] writing me the 11th of October 1876: "Mr Clemens was just in and was in an unusual state of enthusiasm over the first volume, especially its fine style. You may have a picture of his getting up at two o'clock this morning and, encased in a fur overcoat, reading it till daylight."

I cannot enter more fully into the detail of reviews; suffice it to say that two large quarto scrap-books were filled with such notices of the *Native Races* as were sent to me.[17]

All I claimed was faithfully to have gathered my facts, to have arranged them in the most natural manner, and to have expressed them in the clearest language. These were its greatest charms with scholars, and where so few pretentions were made, reviewers found little room for censure.

THUS IT WAS that I began to see in my work a success exceeding my wildest anticipations. And a first success in literature under ordinary circumstances is a most fortunate occurrence. To me it was everything. I hardly think that failure would have driven me from my purpose; but I needed more than dogged persistency to carry me through herculean undertakings.

From the first, success fell upon me like refreshing showers, cleansing my mind and my experiences, and watering all my subsequent efforts.

XV

THE TWO GENERALS

≈

C AME TO THE library the 21st of October 1873 Enrique Cerruti, introduced by Philip A. Roach, editor and senator:
"He speaks Italian, French, Spanish, and English. He can trans-
late Latin. He has been a consul-general and secretary of legation.
He is well acquainted with Spanish-American affairs and the
leading men in those states." The bearer of the letter stood before
me, a man of three or four years under forty, slightly built, with
a long thin face, and a long thin mustache. A drooping Quixotic
melancholy pervaded his entire physique.

Turning him over to Mr Oak, I scarcely gave him a thought.
What specially drew my attention to him was his coming to me
occasionally with something he had secured from an unexpected
source. He used to write frequent and long reviews of my books,
and he had a way of making editors do about as he desired.
Gradually I became interested in this man, and I saw him interest himself more and more in my behalf; with time this interest
deepened into regard, until finally I became strongly attached
to him. This attachment was based on his inherent honesty,
devotion, and kindness of heart, though on the surface he was
bubble and bombast. Within was the strictest integrity, and that
loyalty which makes one literally die for one's friend; without was
fiction, hyperbole, and empiricism.

Henry Cerruti, 1874, courtesy of The Bancroft Library
(Cerruti, Henry—POR2)

Cerruti's oily unctions were laid on so gracefully, so tenderly, and withal so liberally, and with the air of one to whom it made little difference whether you believed him in earnest or not. He was the only man whose flummery, even in homœopathic doses, did not sicken me. To Cerruti, lying was the greatest luxury, a fine art. Falsehood spun itself of its own volition in his whirling brain, and he amused himself by flinging off the fabric from his tongue. It was habit and amusement; to have been forced always to speak the truth would have been to stop the play of the healthful vital organism. He used often to talk to me as long as I would listen, while knowing that I regarded every word he uttered as false. But he took care to make it palatable. If one liked one's praise thickly spread, he enjoyed nothing so much as giving a friend his fill of it. And no one was quicker than he to detect the instant his sweetness nauseated. Every man's face was to Cerruti a barometer, indicating the weather of the mind.

Cerruti liked to parade his illustrious connections, his daring deeds in battle or on the ocean, the offices he had held, the influence he had wielded, and the crushing effect at all times of his enkindled wrath—these were among his constant themes. He well knew that he was not a great man, and never by any possibility could be regarded as such, though he dubbed himself king of his craft; and yet above all things earthly he adored the semblance of greatness.

Notwithstanding his aggressive disposition he was extremely sensitive. His pride was supreme, exposing him to tortures from every defamatory wind. Yet he was as quickly brought from the storm into calm waters. Often with one kind word I have cooled in him a tempest which had been raging perhaps for days. Indeed, here as everywhere in life, clouds were not dispelled by lightning and the thunderbolt, nor by hurling at them other clouds, but by permeating them with soft sunshine.

At first the young men in the library used to laugh at Cerruti; but I pointed to the signal results which he was achieving, and even should he prove in the end knave or fool, success was always a convincing argument. He was keen-scented and bold in his search after historical knowledge. Of all studies, the analysis of human nature is to me the most deeply interesting. And of all such investigations I find none more prolific than the anatomizing of the characters connected with these historical efforts.

Cerruti had power over the minds of men, consummate skill in touching the springs of human action and in winning the wary to his purpose.

Another general: though likewise of the Latin race, with all its stately misdirection, yet broader in intellect, of deeper endowment, and gentler sagacity. Among the Hispano-Californians Mariano de Guadalupe Vallejo[1] deservedly stands first. Born at Monterey the 7th of July 1808, of prominent Castilian parentage, twenty-one years were spent in religious, civil, and military training, after which he took his position at San Francisco as *comandante* of the presidio, collector, and *alcalde*. In 1835 he established the first *ayuntamiento*, or town council, at Yerba Buena cove, where was begun the metropolis of San Francisco, the same year he colonized Sonoma, which ever after was his home.

His face wore usually a contented and often jovial expression, but the frequent short quick sigh told of unsatisfied longings, of vain regrets and lacerated ambitions. And no wonder. For within the period of his manhood he had seen California emerge from a quiet wilderness and become the haunt of embroiling civilization. He had seen arise from the bleak and shifting sand-dunes of Yerba Buena cove a mighty metropolis, the half of which he might have owned as easily as to write his name, but of which there was not a single foot he could now call his own, and where he wandered well nigh a stranger; he had seen the graceful hills and sweet valleys of his native land pass from the gentle rule of brothers and friends into the hands of foreigners, under whose harsh domination the sound of his native tongue had died away like angels' music.

His house in Sonoma, a long two-story adobe, with wing and out-houses, was probably the finest in California. Besides his dusky retainers, who were swept away by diseases brought

General Mariano G. Vallejo, courtesy of The Bancroft Library
(Vallejo, Mariano Guadalupe—POR 2)

upon them by the white man, he had always on the premises
at his command a company of soldiers, and servants without
number. He had there a library and was writing his own history
of California.

Prodigal to a fault were almost all this race of Hispano-
Californians, charging the results of their improvidence meanwhile upon those who had winked at their ruin. Yet this Timon
of Sonoma was never Misanthropos, hating mankind.

XVI

ITALIAN STRATEGY

ENERAL VALLEJO WAS wary; General Cerruti was wily.
Rumor had filled all the drawers and chests at Lachryma
Montis, the residence of General Vallejo at Sonoma, with price-
less documents relating to the history of California, some saved
from the fire which destroyed his dwelling in San José, some
gathered since, and had endowed the owner with singular knowledge in deciphering them and in explaining early affairs.

I had addressed to Sonoma communications several times,
with no tangible result. As Cerruti displayed more and more ability
in gathering material, I directed the Italian to open correspondence
with him, with instructions to use his own judgment in storming
the walls of indifference and prejudice at Lachryma Montis.

License being thus allowed him, Cerruti opened the campaign
by addressing a letter to General Vallejo couched in terms of
true Spanish-American courtesy. He did not fail to state that he
also was a general, though but a consul-general. He had heard of
General Vallejo, as indeed all Bolivia, and Italy, and every other
country had heard of him.

This letter was written in Spanish. General Vallejo's letters
to me were always in Spanish, and mine to him were in English.
But if you wish to be one with a person, you will address him in
his own language. The big fish of Lachryma Montis approached

the bait and took a bite, but did not fail to discover the hook. Still, Cerruti received an invitation to meet the General of Alta California.

So Cerruti went to Sonoma, carrying with him in tongue and temper much that was held in common by the man he visited. Further, the Italian had studied well the character of him he sought to win, and knew when to flatter, and how.

And yet the Spaniard was not duped by the Italian: he was only pleased. When finally the latter veered closer to his errand and spoke of the documents, "I presently saw," said the general to me afterward, "the ghost of Bancroft behind him." Nevertheless, Vallejo listened and was pleased. "After making deep soundings," writes Cerruti in the journal I directed him to keep, "I came to the conclusion that General Vallejo was anxious for some person endowed with literary talents to engage in the arduous task of giving to the world a true history of California....I frankly admitted to him that I had neither the intelligence nor the means for so colossal an enterprise, but assured him that Hubert H. Bancroft," etc. After a brief interview Cerruti retreated with an invitation to dine at Lachryma Montis the next day.

It was a grand opportunity, that dinner party, and we may rest assured our general did not fail to improve it. How well is summed up in his account, where with charming *naïveté* he says: "In such pleasant company hunger disappeared as if by enchantment, and the food placed on my plate was left almost untouched"—in plain English, he talked so much he could not eat.

Next day our expert little general was everywhere, talking to everybody, in barber-shops, beer-saloons, and wine-cellars, in public and private houses, offices and stores. Thus he made the magnate of Sonoma feel that the visitor was at once to become a man of mark in that locality, whom to have as a friend was better for Vallejo than that he should be regarded as opposed to his mission. It was not every day there came to Lachryma Montis such a fascinating fellow as Cerruti, one who paid his board at the Sonoma hotel and his bill at the livery stable; no wonder the Vallejos enjoyed it.

Thus the Italian continued, until a week, ten days, a fortnight, passed without very much apparent headway so far as the mission was concerned. Whenever he spoke of the documents, Vallejo retired within himself. Eventually, Cerruti began more clearly to intimate that the spending of so much time and money in that way would be unsatisfactory to Mr Bancroft. If it was true, as General Vallejo had assured him, that he had nothing, and could not be prevailed upon to dictate his recollections, that was the end of it; he must return to San Francisco and so report.

Now General Vallejo would uncover, little by little, the vast fund of information at his command. Some anecdote would be artfully interwoven with perhaps a dozen historical incidents, showing a fertile field. Soon Vallejo began also to feed Cerruti's appetite with a few papers, granting him permission to take copies of them. There was his office, at the scribe's disposal, where he might write unmolested.

Thus matters continued for two months and more, during which time Oak, Fisher, and myself severally made visits to Sonoma and were kindly entertained at Lachryma Montis. All this time General Vallejo was gaining confidence in my messenger and my work. He could but be assured that this literary undertaking was genuine, solid, searching work.

One day while in a somewhat more than usually confidential mood he said to Cerruti: "I cannot but believe Mr Bancroft to be in earnest, and that he means to give the world a true history of California. I was born in this country; I once undertook to write its history, but my poor manuscript and my house were burned together. I was absent from home at the time. By mere chance my servants succeeded in saving several bundles of documents. I will write to San José for a trunk filled with papers, and of which you may copy for Mr Bancroft what you please."

"But, General," exclaimed Cerruti, overwhelmed by the revelation, "I cannot copy them here. Since you have been so kind as to repose this confidence in me, permit me to take the papers to the library and employ men to copy them; otherwise I might work over them for years."

"Well, be it so," replied the general; "and while you are about it, there are two other chests of documents here which I have never disturbed since the fire. Take them also; copy them as quickly as you can and return them to me. I shall be more than repaid if Mr Bancroft's history proves such as my country deserves."

With June came the two generals to San Francisco. The Vallejo documents were all in the library, and round one of the long tables were seated eight Mexicans copying them. I think this was General Vallejo's first visit to the fifth floor. It was to him an impressive sight. He was attended by Mr Savage, who explained everything, giving in detail what we had done, what we were doing, what we proposed to do.

It was very evident that General Vallejo was pleased. Here was the promise of a work which of all others lay nearest his heart, conducted on a plan which would secure the grandest results.

Cerruti saw his opportunity. Placing himself by his now devoted friend he whispered, "Now is your time, general. If you are ever going to give those papers—and what better can you do with them?—this is the proper moment. Mr Bancroft suspects nothing. There are the copyists, seated to at least a twelvemonth's labor. A word from you will save him this large and unnecessary expenditure, secure his gratitude, and the admiration of all present."

"He deserves them!" was his reply. "Tell him they are his."

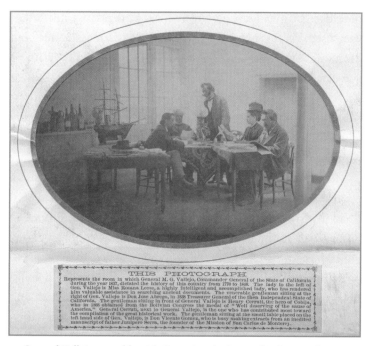

General Vallejo at a table with Cerruti and others at his Sonoma home,
courtesy of The Bancroft Library (1987.025-PIC)

I was literally speechless with astonishment and joy when
Cerruti said to me, "General Vallejo gives you all his papers."

I knew General Vallejo would not stop there. He was slow to
be won, but once enlisted, his native enthusiasm would carry him
to the utmost limit of his ability. From that moment I had not
only a friend and supporter, but a diligent worker. Side by side
with Savage and Cerruti, he alternately wrote history and scoured
the country for fresh personal and documentary information.

It was in April 1874 that Cerruti began writing in Spanish the
Historia de California, dictated by M. G. Vallejo. It was understood
from the first that this history was for my sole use, not to be printed
unless I should so elect, and this was not at all probable. It was

to be used by me in writing my history as other chief authorities were used. Yet this obligation did not in the slightest degree bind me to his views upon any question. I trust I need not say at this late date that I was swayed by no palpable power to one side or another in my writings. I endeavored to prepare his mind for any unwholesome truths which he might see; for most assuredly I should utter them as they came, no matter who might be the sufferer or what the cost.

For several years, while busiest in the collection of material, a good share of my time was taken up in conciliating those whom I had never offended; that is to say, those ancient children, my Hispano-Californian allies, who were constantly coming to grief. Some of them were jealous of me, some jealous of each other; all by nature seemed ready to raise their voices in notes of disputatious woe upon the slightest provocation.

Cerruti and Vallejo continued to work together, visiting residences and churches, to convince the Hispano-Californians to share their documents and memories for Mr Bancroft. Cerruti wrote often amusing and flamboyant narratives of his journeys with General Vallejo. Gradually working south, the two generals did not stop until they had reached Monterey, to the elder a spot pregnant with historical events. The crows cawed history; the cattle bellowed it, and the sweet sea sang it. An interesting chapter could easily be written on Cerruti's report of what he and General Vallejo saw and did during this visit to Monterey; but other affairs equally pressing claim our attention.

XVII

ALVARADO

❧

NEXT AMONG THE Hispano-Californians in historical
importance to Mariano G. Vallejo stood his nephew Juan
B. Alvarado, governor of California from 1836 to 1842.[1] His recollections were regarded by everyone as very important, but exceedingly difficult to obtain. First of all, he must be brought to favor
my undertaking; and as he was poor and proud, in ill health, and
bitter against the Americans, this was no easy matter.

Alvarado had been much less Americanized than Vallejo;
he had mixed little with the new-comers, and could speak their
language scarcely at all. In common with all his countrymen he
fancied he had been badly abused, had been tricked and robbed of
millions of dollars which he had never possessed, and of hundreds
of leagues of land which he had neglected to secure to himself.
To the accursed Yankees were to be attributed all his follies and
failures, all his defects of character, all the mistakes of his life.

Surely one would think so able a statesman, so astute a governor as Alvarado, would have been a match for stragglers into
his territory, or even for the blatant lawyers that followed in their
wake. The same golden opportunities that Vallejo and the rest
had let slip, Alvarado had failed to improve, and the fault was the
ever-to-be-anathematized Yankee. There could be little hope of

success in an appeal to the patriotism of one whose country had fallen into the hands of hated strangers.

On one occasion the governor remarked to the general, "It seems you insist that Mr Bancroft is to be our Messiah, who will stop the mouth of babblers that insult us. I am of the contrary opinion in regard to this, and will tell you why: I do not believe that any American, including a well educated literary man, will contradict what the ignorant populace say of the Californians, from the fact that the *Cholada Gringa*, or Yankee scum, are very numerous, and take advantage of it to insult us, as they are many against few. This is a peculiarity of the American people. To these must be added a great number of Irish and German boors, who unite with them in these assaults. Were we as numerous as the Chinese, it is clear that they would not dare to be wanting in respect to us; but we are merely a few doves in the claws of thousands of hawks, which lay mines charged with legal witcheries in order to entrap us."

However, General Vallejo wrote to Governor Alvarado: "To the eminent writer Hubert H. Bancroft I have given a ton of valuable manuscripts, which have been placed in chronological order, under their proper headings, in order to facilitate the labors in which a dozen literary men of great knowledge are actually occupied....No one has spoken, nor can any one know certain facts as thou and I. All the Americans who have dared to write on this subject have lied, either maliciously or through ignorance."

For a long time Alvarado had been taking historical notes, with a view to writing a history of California. But in his feeble health it was with great difficulty. Every effort was now made to beat down Governor Alvarado's scruples and induce him to dictate a complete history of the country for my use. Finally General Vallejo so far prevailed as to extract the promise desired.

At this juncture came a request from Alvarado. He had a boy for whom he wished to find employment in the store. Anxious to obtain his history, I was ready to do anything which he might reasonably or even unreasonably ask. I sent for the young man, and he was assigned a place in the publishing house.

The boy was but nineteen years of age, and had about as much of an idea of business, and of applying himself to it, as a gray squirrel. A few days afterward I learned that the boy was back at San Pablo, and that a general howl had been raised among his countrymen on account of alleged hard treatment of the boy by the house, that his position had been worse than that of a Chinaman. He was made to work, to wait on people like a servant, to pack boxes, fold papers, and carry bundles. In view of the little need for the boy's services and his lack of skills, he had been assigned a very easy place, and treated with every courtesy. Yet of course the old governor was very angry.

I was greatly chagrined, for I feared all was now lost with Alvarado. It required the utmost efforts of Vallejo and Cerruti to smooth the ruffled pride of the governor. A happier illustration of the irrational puerility of these isolated ancients could not be invented.

I should regard these details too trifling to give them a place here, except as a specimen of every-day occurrences during my efforts to obtain from the Hispano-Californians what they knew of themselves. Taking it altogether, Alvarado's history cost me much time, patience, and money; but I never regretted the expenditure.[2]

Frequently about this time I invited Alvarado, Vallejo, and Cerruti to dine with me at the Maison Dorée, and general good feeling prevailed. Among other things with which the Hispano-Californians were pleased was an article entitled *The Manifest Destiny of California*, which I contributed to the Sacramento

Record-Union, and which was translated and published in a Spanish journal. In writing the article I had not the remotest idea of pleasing any one, and had never even thought of the Californians; but it happened that they were kind enough to like it, and this was fortunate, for it greatly assisted me in obtaining material.

XVIII

CLOSE OF THE
CERRUTI-VALLEJO
CAMPAIGN

≋

For about two and a half years generals Cerruti and Vallejo applied themselves to my work with a devotion scarcely inferior to my own. During the years 1874–6 the time of the two generals was divided between Sonoma, San Francisco, and Monterey, and in making divers excursions from these places.

From Monterey the 6th of January 1875 General Vallejo wrote as follows: "General Cerruti and I go on writing and collecting documents for the history…. Here exist two barrels of old papers belonging to Manuel Castro, which I have not been able to obtain, because it is intended to profit by them. However, if you show yourself indifferent, it is probable that you may obtain them at small expense…. Make use of a very Yankee policy, and within two months you will be the possessor of the richest collection in existence with reference to upper California…."

Another set of important papers they worked on securing together were those of Don Guillermo Hartnell, an Englishman who had come to California at an early date and had married an *hija del pais*, Teresa de la Guerra, by whom he had been made twenty-five times a father.[1] Applying to the widow of Mr Hartnell, General Vallejo received a very welcome reply. The collection of these documents, like so many others, proved to be of great value.

Cerruti, for his part, was unremitting in his labors, seeking and pursuing documents wherever he might be. While the warmest friendship existed between the two generals during the whole of their intercourse, they were not without their little differences. Having accompanied Vallejo to Monterey to collect materials, Cerruti writes in August: "You cannot conceive how pleased I shall be when the work is complete. It has caused me many unhappy moments and many sacrifices of pride." On another occasion he complained: "If I remain in it a month longer I will become an old man. I see only old people, converse as to days gone by. At my meals I eat history; my bed is made of old documents, and I dream of the past. Yet I would cheerfully for your sake stand the brunt of hard times were it not that your agents have wounded me in my pride, the only vulnerable point in my whole nature."

THE GENERALS ALSO sought out the papers of Thomas O. Larkin,[2] United States consul at Monterey when California fell to the United States. Into the hands of such a man as Mr Larkin naturally would fall many important papers. At his death Mr Larkin left a large and very valuable mass of documents and his official correspondence from 1844 to 1849. Charles H. Sawyer, attorney for certain of the heirs of Thomas O. Larkin, and always a warm friend of the library, first called my attention to the existence of these most important archives. Mr Larkin's papers, he assured me, would be most difficult to obtain, since one heir was at the east and another too ill to be seen. At length I learned that Mr Sampson Tams, a very intelligent and accomplished gentleman who had married a daughter of Mr Larkin, had full possession and control of all the Larkin archives. I lost no time in presenting my request. The result was that with most commendable liberality Mr Tams presented me with the entire collection.

While engaged in my behalf at Monterey, General Vallejo's enthusiasm often waxed so warm as almost to carry him away. Now he resolved upon a journey to San Diego, stopping at all the missions. He wrote: "I have endeavored to persuade Cerruti to undertake the journey,…but he has refused to venture into deep water, until the conclusion of the *Historia de California* which I am dictating.…"

The original proposal was for General Vallejo to bring his history down to the year 1846, the end of Mexican domination in California. He wrote: "By the 3d of September I shall have finished the fourth volume.…" He adds: "What I relate is very distinct from what has been hitherto published by writers who have desired to represent as heroes the men who robbed me and my countrymen of our property. American authors desire to excuse those robbers with the pretext that in some cases the 'Bear' captains gave receipts for the articles of which they took forcible possession; but as those receipts were worthless, the Californians have the right to say that the 'Bears,' or a majority of them, were robbers."

War's alarum always threw the mercurial Cerruti into a state of excitement. Even rumors of war between Mexico and the United States, which were of frequent occurrence, were usually too much for his equanimity. I remember one instance, while he was writing at General Vallejo's dictation, in November 1875, news came of serious troubles in the south, and he gave me notice that he should be obliged to abandon his work and fly to the rescue of something or to death. I requested Vallejo to pacify him. Vallejo's arguments were convincing: Cerruti abandoned his project.

The history by General Vallejo being an accomplished fact, the next thing in order was its presentation to the library. This was done, of necessity, with a great flourish of trumpets. The correspondence between General Vallejo and myself in November 1875 reviewing our conjoined accomplishment was published at the time in all the leading journals.

ON THE 9TH of October, 1876, at Sonoma, Enrique Cerruti killed himself. I was east at the time, and the painful intelligence was sent me by General Vallejo. The cause of this deplorable act was losses in mining stocks in relation to gambling debts. He who is tranquillized by a tempest or a war-trumpet quails before the invocation of his own thoughts.

He had talked of suicide for six months previous, but no attention was paid to his threats. He had quarreled and made peace alternately with every person in the library. He resorted to strychnine.

Poor, dear Cerruti! If I had him back with me alive, I would not give him up for all Nevada's mines. His ever welcome presence; his ever pleasing speech, racy in its harmless bluster; his ever charming ways, fascinating in their guileful simplicity, the far-reaching round earth does not contain his like. Alas, Cerruti!

XIX

HOME

There is no happiness in life, there is no misery,
like that growing out of the dispositions
which consecrate or desecrate a home.

—Chapin

I ALMOST DESPAIRED OF ever having a home again. I was
growing somewhat old for a young wife, and I had no fancy
for taking an old one. The risk on both sides I felt to be great. A
Buffalo lady once wrote me: "All this time you might be making
some one person happy." I replied: "All this time I might be making two persons miserable." And yet no one realized more fully
than myself that a happy marriage doubles the resources, and
completes the being which otherwise fails in the fullest development of its intuitions and yearnings. There were certain qualities
I felt to be essential not only to my happiness, but to my continued literary success. Little cared I for the world, with its loves and
hates, whether it regarded me kindly, or not at all. I had a world
within me whose good-will I could command so long as I was
at peace with myself. Out among men I felt myself equal to cope
with any of them. But my home must be to me heaven. There was
no room in my head for discord, nor in my heart for bitterness.

To write well, to do anything well, a right-intentioned humane man must be at peace with the one nearest him. Many a time in my younger married life has a cross word, dropped upon her I loved on leaving my home in the morning, so haunted me while at my business, that I have flung down my work, gone back and dispelled the offence, after which I might return untroubled to my business. Drop into the heart a sweet word, and it will sing all the night long, and all the day; drop into the heart a sharp word, and, rat-like, it will scratch all round, and gnaw, and gnaw!

Nothing so quickly dissipated my ideas, and spoiled a day for me, as domestic disturbances. I had long since accustomed myself to throw off the ever present annoyances of business, even placing my literary peace of mind above the reach of the money-wranglers. But in my home, where my whole being was so directly concerned, where all my sympathies were enlisted and all my affections centred, derangement were fatal.

Hence it was, as the years went by and I found myself day after day alone, after exhaustion had driven me from my writing, that I regarded less hopefully my chances of again having a home.

"I will keep house for you," my daughter used to say.

"But you will marry," was my reply.

"Then we will live with you."

"I would not have you."

"Then you shall live with us."

"'Us' I shall never live with."

"Then I shall not marry!" was the conclusion commonly arrived at.

I had sold my dwelling on California street for several reasons. It was large and burdensome to one situated as I was. Much of my time I wished to spend out of the city, where I would be removed from constant interruption. As long as I had a house I must entertain company. This I enjoyed when time was at my disposal; but drives, and dinners, and late hours dissipated literary effort, and with so much before me to be done, and a score of men at my back whom I must keep employed, I could take little pleasure in pastime which called me long from the library.

My great fear of marrying was lest I should fasten to my side a person who would hurry me off the stage before my task was done, or otherwise so confound me that I never should be able to complete my labors. This an inconsiderate woman could accomplish in a variety of ways—as, for instance, by lack of sympathy in my labors; by inordinate love of pleasure, which finds in society gossip its highest gratification; by love of display, which leads to expensive living, and the like.

Naturally shrinking from general society, and preferring books and solitude to noisy assemblies, like Euripides I was undoubtedly regarded by some as sulky and morose; yet I believe few ever held humanity in higher esteem or carried a kinder heart for all men than I. "When a man has great studies," says George Eliot, "and is writing a great work, he must, of course, give up seeing much of the world. How can he go about making acquaintances?"

Often had I been counselled to marry; but whom should I marry? I must have one competent, mentally, to be a companion—one in whom my mind might rest while out of harness. Then the affection must have something to feed on, if one would not see the book-writer become a monstrosity and turn all into head. As the healthy body seeks food, so the healthy mind faints for friendship, and the healthy heart for love. Nor will love of friends and relatives alone suffice. The solitary being sighs for its mate, its other self.

Whom should I marry, then? The question oft repeated itself. Do not all women delight in the fopperies of fashionable life more than in what might seem to them dry, fruitless toil? Where should love be found of such transforming strength as to metamorphose into a female mind of fair intelligence, and endow its possessor with the same extravagant enthusiasm of which I was possessed?

No; better a thousand times no wife at all than one who should prove unwilling to add her sacrifice to mine for the accomplishment of a high purpose; who should fail to see things as I saw them, or to make my interest hers; who should not believe in me and in my work with her whole soul; who should not be content to make my heart her home, and go with me wherever duty seemed to call, or who could not find in intellectual progress the highest pleasure.

For years my heart had lain a-rusting; now I thought I might bring it out, clean and polish it, and see if it might not be as good as new. It had been intimated by certain critics that I had allowed love of literature to rival love of woman. But this was not true. I was ready at any time to marry the woman who should appear to me in the form of a dispensation.

The higher order of literary character above all things loves simplicity and a quiet life; loves tranquility of mind and a body free from pain; hates interruptions, controversial wranglings, and personal publicity. Minds the wisest, the most exalted, the most finely strung, seem inseparable from some species of madness. Men of genius usually are visionary dreamers; they are often as ingenuous as children, likewise as wayward and as petulant. No wonder women cannot endure them.

The wife of a literary man has her own peculiar troubles, which the world knows not of. Much of the time she is left alone while her husband is buried in his studies. She craves more of his society, perhaps, than he feels able to give her; the theatre, the opera, and evening parties in a measure she is obliged to forego. When talking to her, his speech is not always pleasing. From seeming moroseness he sometimes darts off at the angle of an absurd idea, or indulges in a deluge of dialectics upon society, politics, religion, or any subject which happens to fall under his observation. Besides this he may be at times nervous, fretful, whimsical, full of fault-findings and unjust complaints about the very things to which she has devoted her most careful attention. When we consider all this we cannot much wonder at the proverbial domestic infelicities of authors.

HER LIFE WAS one continuous sparkle. Her face was as a lovely landscape, brightly serene, warmed by all-melting sympathy, and lighted by the glow of intellect. Her voice was like the laughing water. Joyous was her approach, lighting with her sunbeam smile the dismal recesses of reflection; and beaming beautiful as she was without, I found her, as Aristotle says of Pythias, as fair and good within.

Beneath sweet and simple speech in which was no sting, behind a childlike manner in which was no childishness, there was revealed to me, day by day as we walked and talked together, a full developed womanly character, strong, deep, comprehensive. Rallying to my support with ever increasing mental powers, by her ready aid and fond encouragement she doubled my capabilities from the first. For no less in these, than in the good wife's tender trust, lies the strong man's strength.

New Haven had been her home, and of the families of that old university town hers was among the most respected. It was there I first met her, and afterward at Bethlehem, the highest of New England villages. Walking down the dusty road, we turned aside into a rocky field, crossing into a lane which led us to a tangled wood, where seated on a fallen tree, each spoke the words to speak for which we were there. It was the 12th of October, 1876, that I married Matilda Coley Griffing; and from the day that she was mine, wherever her sweet presence, there was my home.

Matilda Coley Griffing Bancroft, from the album *The Founding of a Family*,
courtesy of The Bancroft Library (BANC MSS 73/64 c. v.1)

There was no little risk on her part, in thus committing the
new wine of her love to an old bottle; but that risk she took.

It has been elsewhere intimated that no one is competent to
write a book who has not already written several books. The same

observation might be not inappropriately applied to marriage. No man—I will not say woman—is really in the fittest condition to marry who has not been married before. For obvious reasons, a middle-aged man ought to make a better husband than a very young man. He has had more experience; he should know more, have better control of himself, and be better prepared to have consideration for those dependent upon him for happiness or support.

And the children which come later in the lives of their parents—we might say, happy are they as compared with those who appeared before them. The young husband and father chafes under the new cares and anxieties incident to untried responsibilities which interfere with his comfort and pleasure, and the child must suffer therefrom. Often a newly married pair are not ready at once to welcome children; they are perhaps too much taken up with themselves and the pleasures and pastimes of society. Later in life parents are better prepared, more in the humor it may be, more ready to find their chief pleasure in welcoming to the world successive reproductions of themselves, watching the physical and mental unfolding, and ministering to the comfort and joy of the new and strange little beings committed to them.

There was little lack of sympathy between us, my wife and me, little lack of heart, and help. After the journeying incident to this new relationship was over, and I once more settled at work, all along down the days and years of future ploddings patiently by my side she sat, her face the picture of happy contentment, assisting me with her quick application and sound discrimination, making notes, studying my manuscript, and erasing or altering such repetitions and solecisms as crept into my work.

At White Sulpher springs, and Santa Cruz, where we spent the following spring and summer, on the hotel porches used to sit the feathery-brained women of fashion from the city—used there to sit and cackle all the morning, and all the evening, while we were at our work; and I never before so realized the advantage to woman of ennobling occupation. Why should she be the vain and trifling thing, intellectually, that she generally is? But little cared we for any of them. We were content; nay, more, we were very happy. Rising early and breakfasting at eight o'clock, we devoted the forenoon to work. After luncheon we walked, or rode, or drove, usually until dinner, after which my wife and daughter mingled with the company, while I wrote often until ten or eleven o'clock. In this way I could average ten hours a day; which, but for the extraordinary strength of my constitution, must be regarded twice as much as I should have done.

It was a great saving to me of time and strength, this taking my work into the country. In constant communication with the library, I could draw thence daily such fresh material as I required, and as often as necessary visit the library in person, and have supervision of things there. Thus was my time divided between the still solitude of the country and the noisy solitude of the city.

Never in my life did I work harder or accomplish more than during the years immediately succeeding my marriage, while at the same time body and mind grew stronger under the fortifying influences of home.

FOR A YEAR and more before my marriage I had been under promise to my daughter Kate to go east at the close of her summer school term and accompany her to the centennial exhibition at Philadelphia. This I did, leaving San Francisco the 15th of June 1876, and taking her, with her two cousins and a young lady friend, to the great world's show, there to spend the first two weeks in July. Thence we all returned to New Haven. During a previous visit east I had met Miss Griffing, and I now determined to meet her oftener. After a few weeks in New Haven I proceeded to Buffalo; and thence, after a time, to the White mountains, whither Miss Griffing had migrated for the summer.

Immediately after our marriage we went to New York, Philadelphia, and Washington. My newly wedded pleasure did not, however, render me oblivious to my historical aims. In New York I called on General and Mrs Frémont.[1] They were exceedingly gracious, realizing fully the importance of the work which I was doing, wished particularly to be placed right in history, where they had always been under a cloud, they said, and promised their immediate and hearty coöperation; all of which was idle wind. Why cannot the *soi-disant* great and good always shame the devil?

From New York we went to Washington, and saw Major and Mrs Powell,[2] George Bancroft, Judge Field,[3] Mr Spofford,[4] and many others. After a day at Mount Vernon we returned to Baltimore, there to meet President Gilman, Brantz Mayer,[5] and other friends. Though both of us had seen the exhibition, we could not pass it by upon the present occasion, and accordingly spent a week in Philadelphia.

With new interest Mrs Bancroft now regarded everything pertaining to the Pacific coast. "The Indian trappings in the government building," she writes in her journal begun at this time, "the photographs of the Mound-builders and the Cave-dwellers, the stone utensils and curiously decorated pottery of the Pueblos, the glass photographs of views in Colorado and Arizona, so vividly displaying, with its wild fascinations, the scenery of the west, all seemed suddenly clothed in new charms."

I had long desired a dictation from John A. Sutter.[6] Indeed, I regarded the information which he alone could give as absolutely essential to my history, the first, as he was, to settle in the valley of the Sacramento, so near the spot where gold was first discovered, and so prominent in those parts during the whole period of the Californian Inferno. I knew that he was somewhere in

General John A. Sutter, painting by Stephen W. Shaw,
courtesy of The Bancroft Library (19XX.017-FR)

that vicinity. I telegraphed to San Francisco for his address, and
received in reply, 'Sitig, Lancaster county, Pennsylvania.' After
some search I found 'Sitig' to mean Litiz, and General Sutter
resided there, and was at home.

We travelled up the beautiful valley of the Schuylkill to our
destination. At the Litiz Springs hotel, we were told that the old

gentleman was ill, unable to receive visitors. However, I did not propose to lose my journey to Litiz, this probably my last opportunity for securing this important dictation. I was determined to see the general, if indeed he yet breathed.

When we finally gained egress to the Sutter home, Mrs Sutter showed me into a back parlor and then withdrew, taking my card. Presently, to my great astonishment and delight, the general himself entered at a brisk pace. He appeared neither very old nor very feeble. No one could be in General Sutter's presence long without feeling satisfied that he was an inborn gentleman. He received me courteously, and listened with deep attention to my plan for a history of the Pacific States.

"I have been robbed and ruined," he exclaimed, "by lawyers and politicians. When gold was discovered I had my fortress, my mills, my farms, leagues of land, thousands of cattle and horses, and a thousand tamed natives at my bidding. Where are they now? Stolen! My men were crushed by the iron heel of civilization; my cattle were driven off by hungry gold-seekers; my fort and mills were deserted and left to decay; my lands were squatted on by overland emigrants; and finally I was cheated out of all my property. All Sacramento was once mine."

"General," said I, "this appears to have been the common fate of those who owned vast estates at the coming of the Americans. It was partly owing to the business inexperience of the holders of land grants, though this surely cannot apply to yourself, and partly to the unprincipled tricksters who came hither to practice in courts of law. The past is past. One thing yet remains for you to do, which is to see your wonderful experiences properly placed on record for the benefit of posterity. You will fill an important niche in the history of the western coast. Of certain events you are the embodiment—the living, walking history of a certain time and locality. Often in my labors I have encountered your name, your deeds; and let me say that I have never yet heard the former mentioned but in kindness, nor the latter except in praise."

Tears came to the old man's eyes, and his utterance was choked, as he signified his willingness to relate to me all he knew.

Ten hours a day for the next five days resulted in two hundred pages of manuscript, which was subsequently bound and placed in the library. Forty pages a day kept me very busy, and at night I was tired enough. Meanwhile my devoted bride sat patiently by, sometimes sewing, always lending an attentive ear, with occasional questions addressed to the general.

Thence we proceeded to New Haven, and shortly afterward to San Francisco, stopping at Stockbridge, Buffalo, Granville, Chicago, and Omaha, at all of which places we had friends to visit, before settling finally to work again.

With kind and womanly philosophy Mrs Bancroft on reaching San Francisco did not look about her with that captious criticism so common among newly made California wives, to see if she did not dislike the country. There were some things about the city unique and interesting; others struck her strangely, and some disagreeably. But it seemed never to occur to her to be dissatisfied or homesick. When she married a man, she married him, and there was the end of it, so far as shipping her happiness upon the accidents of his surroundings was concerned. Sweet subtleties! Happier would be the world if there were more of them.

The Palace hotel for a short time was as curious as a menagerie; then it became as distasteful as a prison. We had many pleasant little dinner parties the winter we were there, made up of widely different characters. First there were our nearest and dearest friends, those who had always been to me more than relatives. Then there were the intellectually social; and a third class were Spanish-speaking Californians and Mexicans, among whom were Pio Pico,[7] General Vallejo, Governor Alvarado, Governor

Pacheco,[8] and the Mexican refugees, President Iglesias,[9] and Señores Prieto and Palacio of his cabinet. Mrs Bancroft began the study of Spanish, and made rapid progress; Kate was already quite at home in that language.

It was no part of our plan immediately to domicile ourselves in any fixed residence. Change seemed necessary to my brain, strained as it was to its utmost tension perpetually. It was about the only rest it would take. What is commonly called pleasure was not pleasure so long as there was so much work piled up behind it. It must shift position occasionally, and feed upon new surroundings, or it became restless and unhealthy. Then we had before us much travelling. The vast territory whose history I was writing must be visited in its several parts, some of them many

Lucy, Griffing, Paul, and Philip Bancroft, c. 1886,
from the album *The Founding of a Family*,
courtesy of The Bancroft Library (BANC MSS 73/64 c. v.1)

times. Besides, there was much searching of archives in Europe yet to be done.

Nevertheless, after a year in Oakland, and a winter spent by Mrs Bancroft at New Haven, I purchased a residence on Van Ness avenue, where for many long and busy years echoed the voices of little ones, watched over by a contented mother, whose happy heart was that heavenly sunshine which best pleaseth God. This was indeed Home.

XX

SAN FRANCISCO
ARCHIVES

❧

URING THE FIRST ten years of these Ingatherings and
Industries a dark cloud of discouragement hung over my
efforts, in the form of four or five hundred volumes, with from
seven hundred to nineteen hundred pages each, of original documents, lodged in the office of the United States surveyor-general
in San Francisco. Though containing much on mission affairs,
they constituted the regular archives of the secular government
from the earliest period of Californian history. They were nearly
all in Spanish, and difficult of deciphering.

The United States government took possession in 1846–7 of
all the territorial records that could be found—and in 1851 the
public archives in all parts of California were called in and placed
in charge of the surveyor-general in San Francisco. When E. M.
Stanton[1] came with power from Washington to attend to land
and other affairs of the government, he ordered these archives
bound, although little attention was paid to chronological or
other arrangement. Said Mr Savage to me after a preliminary
examination: "The whole thing is a jumble."

What was to be done? I well knew that I must have before
me all existing material that could be obtained, and I well knew
what 'going through' such a stack of papers signified. No; one of
the chief differences between the old method and the new, was, in
so far as possible, to have all my material together, within instant

reach and not be obliged in the midst of my investigations to go from one library to another note-taking. To be of use to me it must be in my library.

But how get it there? The government would not lend it me, though our benign uncle has committed more foolish acts. There was but one way, the way pursued in smaller operations—copy it.

This transcribing of the archives in the United States surveyor-general's office was the greatest single effort of the kind ever made by me. But there were many lesser labors in the same direction; prominent among these was the epitomizing of the archiepiscopal archives.

I applied to the archbishop of San Francisco for permission to copy them. He wrote to me the following condition, however: "I shall be most happy…to afford every facility to any gentleman you may choose…to copy from any volume…, taking it for granted that…you will let me see before publication what is written on religious matters, lest unintentionally something might be stated inaccurately, which no doubt you would rectify." It is needless to say that neither to the archbishop, nor to any person, living or dead, did I ever grant permission to revise or change my writings. It was my great consolation and chief support throughout my long and arduous career, that I was absolutely free, that I belonged to no sect or party to which I must render account for any expression, or to whose traditions my opinions must bow. Sooner than so hamper myself, I would have consigned my library and my labors to perdition.

Of the value of these archives, Mr Oak observes in writing of California material for history in the public journals of August 1877: "The archives as a whole remain an unexplored and, by ordinary methods, unexplorable waste. Mr Bancroft has not attempted to search the archives for data on particular points; but by employing a large auxiliary force he has substantially transferred their contents to the library. Every single paper of all the 300,000, whatever its nature or value, has been read…; important papers have been copied…. Hardly less important… are the records of the friars in the mission archives.

"Not all the records of early California are to be found in the public offices….The private correspondence of prominent men on public events is quite as valuable a source of information as their official communications. Mr Bancroft has made an earnest effort to gather, preserve, and utilize these private and family archives. There were many obstacles to be overcome; Californians, not always without reason, were distrustful of Gringo schemes; old *papeles* that had so long furnished material for *cigaritos*, suddenly acquired a great pecuniary value…. Yet efforts in this direction have…produced about seventy-five volumes….

"California is a new country; her annals date back but little more than a century; most of her sister states are still younger; therefore personal reminiscences of men and women yet living form an element by no means to be disregarded by the historian. While I am writing there are to be found—though year by year death is reducing their number—men of good intelligence and memory who have seen California pass from Spain to Mexico, and from Mexico to the United States. Many of this class will leave manuscript histories which will be found only in the Bancroft Library."[2]

XXI

HISTORIC
RESEARCHES
IN THE SOUTH

≈

A S I BECAME older in the work, it required of me, both in
person and by proxy, much travel. Southern California was
rightly regarded as the depository of the richest historic material north of Mexico. And the reason is obvious: In settlement
and civilization that region had the start of Oregon by a half
century and more; there were old men there, and family and
public archives. The chief historic adventure in that quarter was
when, with Mr Oak and my daughter Kate, early in 1874 I took
the steamer for San Diego and returned to San Francisco by land.

It was during this journey south that Benjamin Hayes, formerly district judge at Los Angeles, later a resident of San Diego,
and an enthusiastic collector of historic data, not only placed me
in possession of all his collection, but gave me his heart with it.
Beginning with a journal kept while crossing the continent in 1849,
his collection contained manuscripts, scraps from books and early
newspapers, histories written by Father Junipero Serra and Father
Lasuen,[1] pueblo archives from 1829, and manuscript accounts of
Judge Hayes' own travels in various parts of the southern country.
There were some fifty or sixty scrap-books, all stowed in trucks,
cupboards and standing on book-shelves. The question now
was how to transfer this rich mass of historical material to my
library, where, not withstanding the affection with which he who
had labored over the work so long must regard it, I could easily

persuade myself was the proper place for it. Finally, I approached the subject nearest my heart.

"Judge," said I, "your collection should be in my library. There it would be of very great value."

"I am satisfied I shall never write a history," he replied somewhat sadly. "The time has slipped away, and I am now too feeble for steady laborious application.... I know that my material should be added to yours. It is the only proper place for it.... I would gladly give it you, did not I need money so badly...."

"I do not ask you to give me your collection," I returned; "I will gladly pay you for it, and still hold myself your debtor to the same extent as if you gave it."

"It will be some satisfaction to feel that my accumulations are in good hands.... I cannot die and leave them to be scattered here.... With them take all that I can do for your laborious undertaking as long as I live."

And he was as good as his word. Judge Hayes contributed to the packing and shipping of much of his collection, especially his scrap-books of travel and botanical observations. One volume contained about two hundred photographs of places and men in southern California. Taking up one after another of his companion-creations, fondly the little old man handled them; affectionately he told their history. Every paper, every page, was to him a hundred memories of a hundred breathing realities. These were not to him dead facts; they were, indeed, his life. When we began we thought to finish in a few hours, but the obsequies of this collection were not to be so hurriedly performed; surely a volume which had cost a year's labor was worthy a priestly or paternal benediction on taking its final departure. This collection was by far the most important in the state outside of my own.

At night we entered in our journals, of which Mr Oak, Kate, and myself each kept one, the events of the day. Oak and I each wrote about one hundred and fifty pages during the trip, and

Kate forty pages. On our return to San Francisco these journals were deposited in the library.

Departing from San Diego, we called at the missions and saw all the early residents possible, from whom we received valuable information. We then journeyed on to Los Angeles.

Charming Los Angeles! California's celestial city! She of the angels! Indeed, that very day we found a dark-eyed angel, in the shape of a sweet señora with a million dollars and a manuscript. She was close upon forty and a widow. He who had been Abel Stearns had called her wife, and Juan Bandini, daughter.[2] However, when we presented to Mrs Stearns our request for the manuscript of her father, we were informed that it was her mother, Mrs Bandini, to whom we should speak: all the documents of Don Juan belonged to her.

Yes, there was a trunkful of papers left by the late lamented which had never been disturbed, so sighed the Señora Bandini. People said among them was a partially written history; but further than this she knew nothing of the contents of the trunk. However, she could not possibly touch the trunk until the return of her son-in-law, Charles R. Johnson, who was then at San Diego.

It was necessary I should have that material. I saw by this time that I should have more material on northern than on southern California. For a long time the north and the south were in a state of semi-antagonism, and their respective statements would read very differently.

Obviously it would be very much as the son-in-law should say. By inquiry I ascertained the names of those who had influence with him, and these next day I did not fail to see. Others cordially promised their influence in my behalf. Thus for the present I was obliged to leave it. On my return to San Francisco I continued my efforts. I was determined never to let the matter die. The result was that about six months after my first attempt I succeeded in placing the valuable documents of General Bandini, together with his manuscript history of California, upon the shelves of my library.

Andrés Pico[3] was our next essay. His age was sixty-five, or perhaps more. About his mouth played an insidious smile. He took my letter of introduction and assured us: All that was Don Andrés'—his property, his life, his soul—was his friend's and his friend's friends'. All Los Angeles was ours to command.

Well, thought I, this surely is easy sailing. Hayes and Bandini were tempestuous seas beside this placid Pico ocean. At this time I will admit I was too innocent and unsophisticated to cope with the sweet subtleties of Spanish politeness. I never saw Don Andrés again though I sought him diligently.

We continued on our travels to the missions and to seek those who might write their reminiscences. Among them were J. J. Warner, Judge Sepúlveda,[4] and R. M. Widney,[5] who all promised to write, and I am very glad to say these gentlemen were as good as their word. At San Buenaventura we encountered Father Comapala,[6] who also promised to write his experiences for me, having come to the country in 1850, but he did not. He gave me a letter to other old residents, and straightway we hastened to find these walking histories and to wring them out upon our pages.

Mounting the stage at four o'clock P.M., we reached Santa Bárbara at half-past eight. Early next morning we directed our course to the residence of Doctor Alexander S. Taylor, a literary and historical dabster of no small renown in these parts.[7] We found him in his sick-bed with a malady, but our presence was a diversion. I stated briefly the purport of my visit to those parts, and expressed my inability to pass him by without calling, and my regrets at finding him ill. In fact, within two or three years thereafter he was laid low forever. Then I was glad I had seen him. Alas! how rapidly are passing away those who alone can tell us of the past. Within six years after this journey it seemed to me that half the more important men I then met were dead.

I had been told that the Doctor had several volumes ready for publication, but was unable to find a publisher. The conversation turning almost immediately on literary matters, I asked to see the result of his labors. He requested his wife to bring a rough unpainted box, having a lid like a chest, and locked.

"There," said the invalid, turning in bed so that his eyes could rest upon his treasures, "in that box is twenty-five years of my life."

The sick man requested me to examine the contents. The box and all its contents were worth intrinsically nothing. Poor man! In all his pamphlets and scrap-books there was little which we already had not in some shape; hence the value to the library would be but small. I did not regard any of them as of sufficient importance even to ask him his price. The contents of this box he subsequently presented to the society of California pioneers.

Nevertheless it was true that a quarter-century of effort was there, of thought and enthusiasm, of love-labor, the results of a noble life. It *was* a noble life; for a man's life consists in what he attempts to do no less than in what he does.

Our next interview was with the parish priest Padre Jaime Vila, whose residence was attached to the parish church in town. He showed us the mission books. We found here four volumes of *Bautismos*, 1782–1874. The second volume contained the baptisms of aboriginals only. There were besides volumes of *Entierros*, *Matrimonios*, and *Confirmaciones*.

Thence we proceeded to the mission of Santa Bárbara, which unlike any we had hitherto seen, was kept in perfect repair. It was occupied as a Franciscan college and monastery. We found the archives of Santa Bárbara both bulky and important. They consisted of correspondence of the padres, statistics of the several missions, reports, accounts, inventories, and some documents of the pueblo and presidio. They were kept in a cupboard consisting of an aperture about two feet square sunk into a partition wall, and covered with plain folding doors. Father Gonzalez assured me that this cupboard had never been disturbed, as it was apparently not known by any one beyond the mission precincts; we therefore regarded it as a rare discovery, the first real literary bonanza we had unearthed during our excursion.

The archives of this mission seemed to have escaped the fate of all the rest. Besides the papers mentioned, there were papers from trials of persons for polygamy, grammars of the aborigines, and accounts of the different missions.

I asked permission to take the contents of the cupboard to San Francisco to copy, but Father Romo assured me it was impossible. Permission was freely given me, however, to copy as much as I pleased within the mission buildings, of which kind offer I subsequently made avail.

On the 10th of March we left Santa Bárbara by stage, arriving at Ballard's about two o'clock. Early next morning in a farm wagon we drove out to Santa Inés mission to examine the books of Purísima mission located there. Thence, a most uncomfortable night ride in the rain brought us to San Luis Obispo. As we approached the northern end of the line of early ecclesiastical settlements, the missions lay some distance away from the state route, and I concluded to leave those nearest home for another occasion. We all returned, reaching San Francisco the 15th of March, well pleased with our excursion.

IN FOLLOWING UP with the securing of copies and other work that we had initiated on this trip, I had my assistants continue the research in the south of California. One was Edward F. Murray, who proved to be the best; his abstracts on the whole gave satisfaction. To him I gave these instructions among others for the materials we needed: "Personal reminiscences, amusing anecdotes, biographical notes of prominent men and women, historical events, manners and customs of the Californians, amusements, politics, family history, etc.—in fact all that anybody can remember. Go first to the eldest and most intelligent persons; and meantime do all you can to interest the old families in the work."

A further most important work in southern California was performed for me by Mr Thomas Savage in examining archives and collecting narratives. One of these was from José Amador,[8] son of Pedro Amador, one of the soldiers present at the founding of San Diego and Monterey, and for many years sergeant in the San Francisco presidial company. "I found this man of ninety-six years," writes Mr Savage, "who had at one time been wealthy, and after whom Amador county was named, living in great poverty under the care of his youngest daughter, who is married and has many children. He granted my request without asking gratuity, and in six days narrated two hundred and forty pages of original information. I used to take every day something to the children, and occasionally a bottle of Bourbon to warm the old man's heart."

As the history of California progressed it became evident that there were gaps which yet more thorough research alone would fill. Men and women still lived in the south who had taken an active part in or had been witnesses of those troubles between the Californians and Mexicans against the United States occupation. Mr Savage accordingly voyaged in October 1877 to work upon the dictation of Pio Pico, formerly governor of California. He also sought to examine and copy papers of Ignacio Coronel and Manuel Requena,[9] among many other individuals, as well as those at the missions. Throughout the entire expedition Mr Savage was untiring in his efforts, which were not always attended by encouraging success. Yet the next spring he reported, "The results in Santa Bárbara from March 2d to April 4th were about four hundred pages of dictations, over two thousand documents, and two hundred pages of manuscript from the mission books. Much time was spent in vain search for papers not existing." However, Mr Savage was joined by Mr

Murray, who obtained dictations from the American pioneers of that locality, notably from the old trapper Nidever, who came overland to California in 1832.

I have not the space in this chapter to follow Mr Savage further. Many journeys he made for the library, and great were the benefits to history, to California, arising therefrom. His abilities were not surpassed by any.

XXII

HISTORIC
EXPLORATIONS
NORTHWARD

❧

IN COMPANY WITH Mrs Bancroft, on the 30th of April 1878 I sailed in the steamer *City of Panamá*, Captain William Seabury, for Vancouver Island, with the view of returning by land. After five days and nights of tempestuous buffetings, though without special discomfort, we safely landed at Esquimalt, and drove over to Victoria, three miles distant, and found a good hotel.

On setting out from the hotel we met Mr Edgar Marvin, who introduced me to several persons whom I wished to see. To examine public archives and private papers, to extract such portions as were useful in my work, to record and carry back with me the experiences of those who had taken an active part in the discovery and occupation of the country—these, together with a desire to become historically inspired with the spirit of settlement throughout the great north-west, constituted the burden of my mission.

Unfortunately the old Hudson's Bay Company men, whom of all others I wished historically to capture, were many of them politicians. Although they were glad to give me every item respecting their early adventures, they loved office also. But I was persistent. I was determined never to leave the province until my cravings for information should be satisfied.

From many I obtained dictations. Most valuable of all were the reminiscences, amounting in some instances to manuscript volumes, the recollections of those who had spent their lives within this territory, who had occupied important positions of honor and trust, and were immediately identified not only with the occupation and settlement of the country but with its subsequent progress.

James M. Douglas, son of Sir James,[1] granted me free and willing access to all the family books and papers. "Ah!" said everybody, "you should have come before Sir James died. He would have rendered you assistance in value beyond computation." So it is too often with these old men; their experiences and the benefit thereof to posterity are prized after they are beyond reach.

Mrs Bancroft begged permission to assist, and took from one person, a missionary, the Rev. Mr Good, one hundred and twenty foolscap pages descriptive of the people and country round the upper Fraser. In Mr Anderson's narrative, which was very fine, she took special interest, and during our stay in Victoria she accomplished more than any one engaged in the work. Writing in her journal of Mr Good she says, "His descriptions of scenery and wild life are remarkable for vividness and beauty of expression. His graphic pictures so fascinated me that I felt no weariness, and was almost unconscious of effort."

The last day of May we crossed to Port Townsend. At every move a new field opened. Judge James G. Swan,[2] ethnologist, artist, author, was there ready to render me every assistance, which he did by transferring to me his collection, the result of thirty years' labor, and supplementing his former writing by other experiences. Poor fellow! The demon Drink had long held him in his terrible toils, and when told that I was in town he swore he would first get sober before seeing me. How many thousands of our pioneer adventurers have been hastened headlong to perdition by the hellish comforter! Major J. J. H. Van Bokkelen was there, and after giving me his dictation presented to Mrs Bancroft a valuable collection of Indian relics, which he had been waiting twenty years, as he said, to place in the hands of some one who would appreciate them.

Immediately upon our arrival at Olympia we were waited upon by the governor, Mrs Ferry, and Elwood Evans, historian of this section. "I had hoped," said he, "to do this work myself, but your advantages are so superior to mine that I cheerfully yield. I only wish to see the information I have gathered during the last thirty years properly used, and that I know will in your hands be done."

And so the soul of this man's ambition, in the form of two large cases of invaluable written and printed matter on the Northwest Coast, was shipped down to my library, of which it now constitutes an important part. To call such a one generous is faint praise.

At Portland we found ready to assist us many warm friends, among them S. F. Chadwick, then governor of Oregon. Mrs F. F. Victor, whose writings on Oregon were by far the best extant, and whom I wished much to see, was absent. On my return to San Francisco I wrote offering her an engagement in my library, which she accepted, and for years proved one of my most faithful and efficient assistants.

We were informed that the annual meeting of the Oregon pioneers' association was to open immediately in Salem. Dropping our work at Portland, we proceeded at once to the capital, and entered upon the most profitable five days' labor of the entire trip; for there we found congregated from the remotest corners of the state the very men and women we most wished to see, those who had entered that region when it was a wilderness, and had contributed the most important share toward making the society and government what it was.

We worked with a will, day and night; and the notes there taken, under the trees and in the buildings about the fair-grounds, at the hotel, and in private parlors and offices, make a huge pile of historic lore when written out as it was on our return to San Francisco. There was John Minto,[3] eloquent as a speaker and writer, with a wife but little his inferior; the women, indeed, spoke as freely as the men when gathered round the camp fires of the Oregon pioneers' association. Mrs Minto had to tell how women lived, and labored, and suffered, and died, in the early days of Oregon; how they clothed and housed themselves, or rather, how they did without houses and clothes during the first wet winters of their sojourn; how an admiring young shoemaker had measured the impress of her maiden feet in the mud, and sent her as a present her first Oregon shoes. Surely I met at Salem two or three hundred prominent Oregonians.

On our way back to Portland we stopped at Oregon City, where I obtained more recitals. I cannot fail specially to mention the remarkable dictations given me by Judge Deady[4] and Judge Strong,[5] each of which constitutes a history of Oregon in itself.

After a visit to the Dalles, overland by rail to San Francisco was next, with private conveyance over the Siskiyou mountains, a trip I had long wished to make, and we enjoyed every hour of it. At Jacksonville I sat through the entire night, until my carriage called for me at break of day, taking a most disgusting dictation from the old Indian-butcher John E. Ross. This piece of folly I do not record with pleasure.

I never regarded it in the light of personal favor for those having material for history, or information touching the welfare of themselves, their family, or the state, to give it me to embody in my work. However, even among the many who contributed, there was singular lack of consideration and cooperation. I might go to any amount of trouble, spend any amount of money, yet it never seemed to occur to them to furnish me their dictation at their expense instead of mine. Moneyed men of San Francisco have growled to me by the hour about their great sacrifice of valuable time in telling me their experiences. I always felt that the obligation was all the other way; that my time was spent for their benefit rather than for my own. As a matter of course, my object was to benefit neither myself primarily nor them, but to secure to the country a good history.

XXIII

FURTHER
LIBRARY DETAIL

≫

I F THE HISTORY of my literary efforts be worth the writing, it is in the small particulars of every-day labors that the
reader will find the greatest profit. Regular business hours were
kept in the library, namely, from eight to twelve, and from one
to six. Smoking was freely allowed. Certain assistants desired to
work evenings and draw extra pay. This was permitted in some
instances, but always under protest. Nine hours of steady work
were assuredly enough for one day, and additional time seldom
increased results; so, after offering discouragement for several
years, a rule was established abolishing extra work.

Since civilization has assumed such grand proportions and
the accumulated experiences of mankind have become so bulky,
it is comparatively little that one man, with his own brain and
fingers, can accomplish. He who would achieve great results must
early learn to utilize the brain and fingers of others. As applied to
the industrial life, this has long been understood; but in regard
to intellectual efforts, particularly in the field of letters, it has been
regarded as less practicable, and by many impossible.

The system of note-taking, as perfected by Mr Nemos, my
research assistant, was as follows: The notes were written on half
sheets of legal paper, always leaving a space between notes so that
they could be torn apart. The notes when separated and arranged

were filed by means of paper bags, on which were marked subject and date, and the bags numbered chronologically and entered in a book.

After the notes had been used, with all printed matter bearing on the subject, they were returned to the bags to be pasted on sheets of strong brown paper, folded and cut to the required size. These, bound and lettered, would make some three hundred books. In this way it was deemed best to present the subject much more in detail than the printed volumes.[1]

Then, the assistant arranged references and notes in a chronologic order. Notes on commerce, education, geography, etc., were then joined to such dates or occurrences as called for their use: geography coming together with an expedition into a new country. This preliminary grouping was facilitated by the arrangement of the notes for the particular section of territory. And so the systematic extracting and refining of information continued on, with all perspectives on a topic included. By this means I obtained a sort of bird's-eye view of all evidence on the topics for my history as I took them up one after the other in accordance with my own order and plan for writing.

In November 1872 I engaged a copperplate engraver, and from that time till the *Native Races* was completed I had engravers at work at the Market-street end of the library.

About this time I studied the question of the origin of the native Americans, to find a place in some part of the *Native Races*, I did not know then exactly where. When I began this subject I proposed to settle it immediately; when I finished I was satisfied that neither I nor any one else knew. I found some sixty theories, one of them about as plausible or as absurd as another, and hardly one of them capable of being proved or disproved. I concluded to spread them all before my readers, not as of any intrinsic value, but merely as curiosities; and this I did in the opening chapter of volume v. of the *Native Races*.

A FIRE WHICH BROKE out in November 1873 in the basement of the western side of the building seemed likely for a moment suddenly to terminate all our labors. At one time there appeared not one chance in ten that the building or its contents would be saved; but thanks to a prompt and efficient fire department, the flames were extinguished, with a loss of twenty-five thousand dollars only to the insurance companies.

The time was about half-past five in the evening. I had left the library, but my assistants were seated at their tables writing. To have saved anything in case the fire had reached them would have been out of the question. They were so blinded by the smoke that they dared not trust themselves to the stairs, and it was with difficulty they groped their way to a ladder at one side of the room, which led to the roof, by which means they mounted and emerged into the open air. In case the building had burned, their escape would have been uncertain. No damage was done to the library, and all were at their places next morning; but it came home to me more vividly than ever before, the uncertainty, not to say vanity, of earthly things. Had those flames been given five minutes more, the Bancroft Library, with the Bancroft business, would have been swept from the face of earth; the lore within would have been lost to the world, and with it mankind would have been spared the infliction of the printed volumes which followed. Thus would have ended all my literary attempts. In the burning of the library, great as would have been my loss, that of posterity would have been greater.

I N 1875 I DECLINED the republican nomination for member of congress. There were ten thousand ready to serve their country where there was not one to do my work in case I should abandon it. In March 1876 Mr John S. Hittell came to the library and asked permission to propose my name as honorary member of the Society of California pioneers. The rules of the society were such that none might be received as regular members who reached this country for the first time after the 31st of December 1849. While I was duly grateful for the honor conferred, I was unable to perceive how any alliance, even in mere name or imagination, could be formed which would be of the slightest benefit to them or to me.

The 15th of October 1875 saw the *Native Races* completed; but long before this, note-taking on the *History of the Pacific States* had been begun. It is an immense territory, this western half of North America; it was a weighty responsibility, at least I felt it to be such, to lay the foundations of history, for all time, for this one twelfth part of the world.

The task of making references as well as that of taking out material was equivalent to five times the labor of writing; so that at this work, and preparing the material in the rough, I found no difficulty in keeping employed fifteen to twenty persons; for example, in taking out the material for California history alone, eight men were occupied for six years. Counting those engaged on such work as indexing newspapers, epitomizing archives, and copying manuscript, I have had as many as fifty men engaged in library detail at one time. I then found myself at the head of a corps of thoroughly competent and trained assistants, very different in points of knowledge and ability from the untutored and unskilled workmen who assisted me at the beginning of these undertakings. They, as well as I, had learned much, had gained much experience in abstracting material for history, and in printing and publishing books. For five years our minds had been dwelling on these things, and on little else. Our whole intellectual being had, during these years, become saturated with the subject.

The library was moved to Valencia street the 9th of October 1881, and type-setting was begun on the history the following day. Although opposed in this move by several of my friends, I persisted. I was becoming fearful lest it would never be put into

type; lest I should not live to complete the work. I was determined to do what I could in that direction while life lasted. My
health at this time was poorer than ever before, and my nerves
were by no means quieted by reading one day an article on the
business, submitted to me by Mr Hittell for his *Commerce and
Industries*, in which he took occasion to remark of my literary
undertakings: "The scale on which he has commenced his work
is so comprehensive that it is doubtful whether he will be able
to complete it even if he should reach the age of three score and
ten, with continuous prosperity and good health." I thereupon
resolved to complete it, to postpone dying until this work was
done, and I immediately ordered a dozen compositors to be put
upon the manuscript.

Further than this, not only would I print, but I would publish. I had no delicacy now in placing the imprint of the firm on
my title-plates. The world might call it making merchandise of
literature if they chose: I knew it was not, that is to say in a mercenary sense. So I engaged Mr Nathan J. Stone, lately of Japan
but formerly of our house, a man of marked ability, of much
experience in our establishment and elsewhere, to devote himself to the publication and sale of my books. Transferring to him
the business connected therewith, I went on with my writing
more vigorously if possible than before. I requested the mayor
and the governor to visit the library, inspect the work, and then
give me a certificate, expressing their belief in the completion
of the work as then promised, which was at the rate of three or
four volumes a year. I took better care of my health than before,
determined to piece out my life to cover the time I now calculated
would be required to finish the work. Lastly I revised my will to
provide the necessary funds, and appointed literary executors, so
that my several books should be completed and published even
in the event of my death. Strange infatuation, past the compre-
hension of man! Of what avail this terrible straining, with my

body resolved to dust and my intellect dissipated in thin air! For all that, I would abridge my life by twenty years, if necessary, to complete the work; why, I cannot tell.

There is something extremely fascinating to me in the printing of a book. The metamorphoses of mind into manuscript, and manuscript into permanent print; the incarnation of ideas, spreading your thoughts first upon paper and then transfixing them by the aid of metal to the printed page, where through the ages they may remain, display a magic beside which the subtleties of Albertus Magnus[2] were infantile.

Originally I thought of the history only as one complete work, the volumes to be written and published in chronological order; but later it occurred to me that there was too great a sweep of territory, climates and governments too several and diverse, for me arbitrarily to cement them in one historical embrace. Many persons would like a history of one or more of the countries, but would not care for them all. Therefore I finally concluded to write and number the volumes territorially, and yet maintain such chronological order as I was able; that is, I would begin with Central America, that part coming first in order of time, and bring the history of those states down to date. The works might then be lettered under both titles and the purchaser be given his choice; or he might prefer to include the *Native Races* and the supplemental volumes under the yet more general title of *Bancroft's Works*. Thus would simplicity and uniformity be preserved, and purchasers be satisfied.

Another work of the highest importance later forced itself upon me, and took its place among my labors as part of my history. This was the lives of those who had made the history, who had laid the foundations of empire on this coast upon which future generations were forever to build. Thus far a narrative proper of events had been given, while those who had performed this marvelous work were left in the background. Every one felt that they deserved fuller treatment, and after much anxious consideration of the subject, there was evolved in my mind a separate section of the history under title of *Chronicles of the Builders of the Commonwealth.*

Much of the labor on these volumes was performed at my home, where was the sweetest and most sympathizing assistant a literary drudge ever had, constant in season and out of season, patient, forbearing, encouraging, cheering. Many a long day she has labored by my side, reading and revising; many womanly aspirations she has silenced in order to devote her fresh, buoyant life to what she ever regarded as a high and noble object. God grant that she and our children may long live to gather pleasant fruits from these Literary Industries, for I suspect that in this hope lies the hidden and secret spring that moves the author in all his efforts.

XXIV

MY METHOD OF
WRITING HISTORY

≈

M Y SYSTEM OF historical work requires a few words
of explanation, since not a little of the criticism, both
favorable and unfavorable, has been founded on the erroneous
conception of its nature. My system applies only to the accumulation and arrangement of evidence upon the topics of which I
write, and consists in the application of business methods and
the division of labor to those ends. By its aid I have attempted to
accomplish in one year what would require ten years by ordinary
methods. I tunnel the mountain of court records and legal briefs,
bridge the marsh of United States government documents, and
stationing myself at a safe distance in the rear, hurl my forces
against the solid columns of two hundred files of California newspapers. I claim that mine is the only method by which all the
evidence on a great subject or on many smaller subjects can be
brought out.

In my literary work, at every turn, I found myself deriving
the largest benefits from my business experience. Before I had
been engaged in my historical labors for five years I found my
new work broadly planned and fairly systematized. Accustomed
to utilize the labors of others, I found no difficulty in directing a
small army of workers here. I have always encouraged among my

assistants a free expression of their own ideas, and have derived the greatest benefit from frequent conversations and discussion with them on special topics.

Moreover, I found myself as free as might be from prejudices, though this, I believe, is the opinion of the wildest fanaticism concerning itself; free from sectarianism and party bias, and from the whole catalogue of isms, some of which are apt to fasten themselves on immature minds and there remain through life. I found myself with no cause to battle for, no preconceived rights or wrongs to vindicate or avenge, no so-called belief to establish, no special politics to plead. I had no aim or interest to present aught but the truth; and I cared little what truth should prove to be when found, or whether it agreed with my conceptions of what it was or ought to be. If wealth increased life, there would be some sense in struggling for it. But this is not so: it absorbs life. Only the multiplication of mind multiplies life; and it is in the exercise of this privilege alone that man is better than a brute.

If the commercial man has a cultivated intellect, he has an unfailing resource within himself. Yet absolute retirement from an active and successful business life which he loves, even to a purely intellectual life which he loves better, may not be always the best a man can do. The strains of study and writing are so severe upon the nerves that at times business may be recreation—that is, if the business is well systematized and successful, with plenty to do, with plenty of capital, and without haste, anxiety, or worry.

Writes Mr Harcourt to me the 4th of April 1877, "This notable success is partly owing to the wise and far-sighted system you have adopted of leaving to others the drudgery that is inseparable from literary labor, and thereby keeping your own energies fresh for the part that is expected of genius. You have carried the progressive spirit of the age into a quarter where it is least expected to be found, for you have applied machinery to literature, and have almost done for book-writing what the printing-press did for book dissemination."

After all that may be said of inventions and systems, or even of ability, work, work was ever my chief dependence. I found fastened upon me as part of my nature habits of application and perseverance from which I could not tear myself if I would. I was wound up by my mother to work; and so wound that the running down should be with the last tick of time.

XXV

FURTHER INGATHERINGS

≫

WITH GOETHE I might truly say at this juncture that the little I had done seemed nothing when I looked forward and saw how much remained to be done. Whatever else I had in hand, never for a moment did I lose sight of the important work of collecting. I regarded with deep longing the territory marked out, where so much loss and destruction were going on, and at such a rapid rate. My desires were insatiable. So thoroughly did I realize how ripe was the harvest and how few the laborers, how rapidly was slipping from mortal grasp golden opportunity, that I rested neither day nor night, but sought to secure from those thus passing away, all within my power to save before it was too late. With the history of the coast ever before me as the grandest of unaccomplished ideas, I gathered day by day all scraps of information upon which I could lay my hands.

Utah was not the easiest of problems with which to deal historically. Not that I had any hesitation about treating the subject when once I came to it, but prejudice against the Mormons was so strong and universal, and of such long standing, that anything I could say or do short of wilful and persistent vituperation would not satisfy the people. This with me was out of the question. Hate is insane; injustice is the greatest of crimes. At the outset in my writings I was determined that no power on earth should sway me from telling the truth. I would do all parties and sects justice, according to the evidence, whatsoever pandemonium of criticism or unpopularity such a course might lead me. In treating of the Chinese, a fair statement would satisfy neither one side nor the other; in treating of Utah, I well knew that strict impartiality would bring upon me the condemnation of both Mormons and gentiles. If this, then, was the test of truth and fair dealing, I must subject myself to the censure of both sides; at all events, as had been my invariable custom in regard to nationalities, and religions, social and political prejudices, I would not write for the approbation of one side or the other.

The Mormons possessed stores of information that I desired. Orson Pratt,[1] historian and church recorder, intimated to me that if I would print "without mutilation" what he should write, he would furnish a complete history of Utah. This only showed that they were wholly mistaken in the character of my work. It was in this state of mind that I indited the following from an epistle of the 12th of January, 1880: "We of the Pacific slope are now at the turning-point between civilization's first generation in this domain and the second. The principal facts of our history we can now obtain beyond a peradventure. Some are yet living, though these are fast passing away, whose adventures, counsels, and acts constitute a part of early history. There are men yet living who helped to make our history, and who can tell us what is better than their sons, or than any who shall come after them.... Twenty years ago many parts of our territory were not old enough to have a history; twenty years hence much will be lost that may now be secured."

Mr Franklin Richards came to represent Mr Pratt, and I found him everything I could desire. He was of singularly humane and benevolent mien, and, except on points pertaining to his faith, possessed of broad views and liberal ideas. He held to his faith as other men hold to theirs, and I fully accorded him this liberty. It did not concern me what were his ideas regarding the divine mission of Joseph Smith,[2] or the inspiration of the book of Mormon; and if with three or six women he had entered into marriage relations, I did not propose to follow public sentiment and fight him for it. In fact each of us entertained too much respect of the other to attempt coercion or conversion.

Mr and Mrs Richards spent the greater part of July in San Francisco, most of the time as my guests. While Mr Richards was giving a fortnight's dictation to my reporter at the library, Mrs Richards imparted to Mrs Bancroft much information concerning female life and society in Utah, which was also preserved in writing.

THESE INGATHERING EXPERIENCES were not always smooth and pleasant. Much that was annoying or exasperating has been left unsaid. There is one case, however, that should not be passed unnoticed.

All their lives John Charles and Jessie Frémont had been railing against the world, complaining of the injustice done them. Their own conduct had always been beyond reproach; only the rest of mankind were desperately wicked. For thirty years they had clamored for justice.

I called upon them, explained fully the character of my work, and invited them to place before me the data for a correct statement of their grievances. They affected great interest. Mrs Frémont, as the regnant avenger of her husband's wrongs, vowed she would bring John Charles to the front, open his mouth, and catch the fury flowing thence upon her paper; likewise John Charles roused himself to say it should be done.

Thus matters stood for two or three years, the Frémonts always promising but never performing. I could not understand it; it seemed to me so grand an opportunity to accomplish what they had always pretended to covet, namely, their proper place in history. At last it came out: they wanted money. If, indeed, they were in the possession of knowledge belonging to their country, it could scarcely be called praiseworthy to keep it back for a price, when they had been, the greater part of their lives, fed and clothed at public expense.

I would here state that I had never paid for original historical testimony. Thousands of dollars had I expended in committing such knowledge to writing, but to pay the narrator money, except by way of charity, I never could do. Intellectual wealth can only exist as the common property of the body social.

Notwithstanding all that had been done up to this time, I felt I should have more of the testimony of eye-witnesses. Particularly among the pioneers of and prior to 1849, and among the native Californians inhabiting the southern part of the state, there was information, difficult and costly to obtain, but which I felt could not be dispensed with.

Mr Oak suggested we should make one more appeal, one final effort, before finishing the note-taking for California history; and to this end, the 25th of August 1877, he addressed over his own signature a communication to the San Francisco *Bulletin*, reviewing what had been done and sketching what was still before us.

Extra copies of this article were printed and sent to school-teachers and others throughout the coast, with the request that they should call upon such early settlers as were within their reach and obtain from them information respecting the country at the time of their arrival and subsequently. For writing out such information, for one class would be paid twenty cents a folio, and for another less desirable class and one more easily obtained, fifteen cents a folio was offered. Not less than five thousand direct applications were thus made, and with the happiest results. Thus I went over the ground repeatedly, and after I had many times congratulated myself that my work of collecting was done; in truth I came to the conclusion that such work was never done.

XXVI

PRELIMINARY AND
SUPPLEMENTAL
VOLUMES

～

A S I HAVE elsewhere remarked, the soul and centre of this
literary undertaking was the *History of the Pacific States*;
the *Native Races* being preliminary, and the *California Pastoral,
Inter Pocula, Popular Tribunals, Essays and Miscellany,* and *Literary Industries* supplemental thereto. To the history appears
a biographical section entitled *Chronicles of the Builders of the
Commonwealth.*

H. H. Bancroft writing at his desk, from the album *The Founding of a Family,*
courtesy of The Bancroft Library (BANC MSS 73/64 C. V.1)

There was with me a constant anxiety to press forward my writing; I had but a short time to live and very much to do. But when I saw how my first work was received, and how I should stand with the literary world after its publication, I determined to print nothing more for several years. I had several reasons for adopting such a resolution.

First, no one ever realized more fully than myself that it takes time and work to make a good book. Second, I thought it better to give the public a little rest. My books were heavy and expensive, and to issue them too rapidly might cheapen them in the eyes of some. Right well, too, I knew that often literary failure had been followed by literary success and *vice versa*. Among other lessons learned while writing this work was never to come too near the object about which you wish to write well.

XXVII

BODY AND MIND

≋

S OME STRENGTH AND stores of health had been laid in for me, thanks to my father who gave me first an iron constitution, and supplemented it with that greatest of earthly blessings, work, in the form of plowing, planting, harvesting, and like farm occupation. I doubt if in all the range of educational processes, mental and physical, any equals the farm. Later in life it was only by excessive physical exercise that I could bear the excessive strain on my nervous system. By hard riding, wood-sawing, long walks and running, I sought to draw fatigue from the over-taxed brain, and fix it upon the muscles.

On seating myself to years of literary labor, I sought in vain some intellectual charm in muscle making. Though I loved nature, delighting in the exhilaration of oxygen and sunlight, and in the stimulus of contrary winds, yet so eager was I to see progress in the long line of work I had marked out, that only the most rigid resolution enabled me to do my duty in this regard. I felt that I had begun my historical efforts late in life, and there was much that I was anxious to do before I should return to dust. In my hours of recreation I worked as diligently as ever. I sought such exercise as hardened my flesh in the shortest time.

A sound mind in a sound body is only secured by giving both body and mind their due share of labor and of rest. "Extreme activity of the reflective powers," says Herbert Spencer, "tends to deaden the feelings, while an extreme activity of the feelings tends to deaden the reflective powers."

Worry is infinitely more consuming than work. Doctor Carpenter charges worry and consequent mental strain as the cause of the premature death of business and professional men of the present day. The chafings of the mind are far worse than those of the body. He who would live long and perform much mental work must fling care to the winds.

For years it was my custom to rise at seven, breakfast at half past seven, and write from eight until one, when I lunched or dined. The afternoon was devoted to recreation and exercise. Usually I would get in an hour's writing before a six o'clock tea or dinner, as the case might be, and four hours afterwards, making ten hours in all for the day; but interruptions were so constant and frequent, that including the many long seasons during which I hermited myself in the country, where I often devoted twelve and fourteen hours a day to writing, I do not think I averaged more than eight hours a day, taking twenty years together.

When I first began to write, composing was a very labored operation. But gradually I came to think less of myself and the manner of expression, and more of what I was saying. Sometimes a flood of thought would come rushing in upon me, like a torrent overwhelming its banks, and I would lose the greater part of it; at other times so confused and slothful would be my brain, that in turning over the leaves of my dictionary I would forget the word I was looking for. This was more particularly the case during the earlier part of my literary career; later my mind became more tractable, and I never waited for either ideas or words.

In the free and natural flow of ideas in writing, the position must be neither too easy nor too constrained; as the former tends to inanity, while the latter distracts the mind from the subject in hand and fixes it upon muscular discontent. Thought is sometimes a little freaky. Change of room, a rearrangement of books and papers often breaks the current of thought, and severs the subtle connection between mind and its surroundings. Seating myself at my table in the morning and seeing all my papers as they were left, I take up the thread where I dropped it the night before.

Interruptions are fatal to good work. While at the library my time was greatly broken by callers. Often in a fit of desperation I have seized a handful of work and rushed into the country, where I could count with some degree of certainty upon my time. Truly, says Florence Nightingale, "I have never known persons who exposed themselves for years to constant interruptions who did not muddle away their intellects by it at last."

In January, 1876, I left San Francisco in one of these moods suddenly, and under a sense of something akin to despair. It seemed as though my work would stretch out to all eternity. I stepped aboard the boat and that night slept at my father's. During the next six weeks of a simple life, without interruptions, I accomplished more in a literary way than during any other six weeks of my life. I worked from ten to twelve hours, and averaged twenty pages of manuscript a day, rode two hours, ate heartily, drank from half a bottle to a bottle of claret or sherry before retiring, and smoked four or five cigars daily.

There is no end to the rules and regulations I have made to govern my writing. I believe in them. Yet I do not hesitate to break my rules whenever occasion seems to demand it. Self-knowledge is the sum of all knowledge.

It has seemed to me at times as if I was filled with the poetic instinct but without poetic expression; that my poor inspiration was born dumb. Often after the close of business have I walked out alone, up one street and down another, for hours and far into the night, star-gazing, thinking, communing, the dim and palpitating light singing me a soul-song, and playing with the dim and palpitating light which so feebly filled my brain.

Not unfrequently the most unaccountable freaks of indisposition seize the steady literary worker. Even the iron constitution of Mr Oak was not free from them, and indeed toward the end he almost broke down. On one occasion he wrote me on the 3d of April, 1877, "I cannot sleep....I find it impossible to fix my mind on any definite point of my work." Rest was all that he needed, however, for after a few weeks in the country he was himself again.[1]

As regards society and solitude both are necessary, but here as elsewhere extremes should be avoided. The tendency with me during my periods of severest labor, as with every hard-worker, was more and more towards aloneness. With hundreds of highly intellectual persons on every side of me, there were few whose tastes or habits led them in the direction of my labors. As a rule I found books more profitable than social intercourse, so much so that the time spent walking with men and women seemed to me lost.

Say what you will of the benefits of social intercourse, an intellectual man can spend but little time in unintellectual society except to his disadvantage. To a sensible person current society is a lame affair; an intellectual man finds it specially insipid.

XXVIII

EXPEDITIONS TO MEXICO

⌇

Having read and written so much about Mexico, it was but natural that I should wish to go there. I had completed the history of all that region, with abundance of material, down to the year 1800, and for the present century I knew that there existed houses full of information which I did not possess.

Accordingly on the 1st day of September, 1883, I set out, accompanied by my daughter Kate and a Mexican servant, for the great city of the table-land, proceeding via San Antonio and Laredo, Texas. I took copious notes of everything I encountered, all of which I utilized at good advantage in Volume vi of my *History of Mexico*. The chief object of my visit was to ascertain about libraries and literature, and the amount and quality of material for history existing in the republic.

On reaching the city of Mexico, I took up my quarters at the hotel Iturbide, where I remained four months, ransacking the city, and making excursions in various directions. I had letters of introduction and at once sent them out, requesting interviews. When I spoke with the American minister Mr Morgan, he said, "I cannot see why you want to make the acquaintance of these people. If it is to be entertained by them, you will be disappointed. Here am I these three or four years representing the great American republic, and they pay not the slightest attention to me."

"My dear sir," I said, "it is the last thing I desire—to be entertained. I come to Mexico for a far different purpose."

For about two weeks my time was chiefly occupied in making and receiving calls. Indeed, I met so many who treated me so cordially, seeming to count it a pleasure to serve me, that I have not the space to devote to them which their merits deserve. One of the first to visit me was Ygnacio M. Altamirano,[1] one of the chief literary men in Mexico, who boasts his pure Aztec blood uncontaminated by any European intermixture. Altamirano divided the leading literary honors of the capital with Alfredo Chavero,[2] who was also quite talented. Another very agreeable *littérateur* was Ireneo Paz,[3] member of congress and proprietor of *La Patria*, on the front page of which Señor Paz did me the honor to place my portrait, with a biographical notice, reviewing my books.

I found in the prominent lawyer and statesman Francisco L. Vallarta a most serviceable friend. Then Manuel Romero Rubio, father-in-law of the late president, introduced me to Porfirio Diaz,[4] and he to President Gonzalez.[5] From General Diaz, the foremost man in the republic, I took a two weeks' dictation, employing two stenographers, and yielding 400 pages of manuscript. Naturally, during this time, and subsequently, I became well acquainted with the Diaz family, dining frequently there and with the father of the charming wife of the president, whose home was one of the most elegant in the capital.

Porfirio Diaz appears more American than Mexican. He has had his triumphs; perhaps his humiliations are yet to come. Few great men escape them toward the end of their career; indeed they seem necessary, in the economy of politics, to terminate the too ambitious man's efforts, whose pretensions otherwise would know no bounds.

The two great receptacles of knowledge, ancient and modern, historical, scientific, and religious, in the Mexican capital, and which make the heart of the student, investigator, or collector quail before them, are the Biblioteca Nacional, or national library, and the Archivo General y Público de la Nación, or national archives. At the national archives, the section on history relating to California and the internal provinces I have largely copied. Of this institution I obtained direct and important information, far more than I can print.

I also visited the municipal archives of the district of Mexico, which consists of documents accumulated during the past 200 years. Among libraries of historic interest were the Biblioteca Popular del 5 de Mayo, church libraries, and later the public library of Toluca. Indeed, Mexico has many libraries containing important historic data. There are many rare and valuable books throughout the republic; but of the class commonly called rare by collectors and bibliographers, valuable only as specimens of early printing, most of these have been carried away.

All the while I was in Mexico I gathered books, took dictations, wrote down my thoughts and observations. With some difficulty I succeeded in obtaining enough of the leading journals published in Mexico since 1800 to make a continuous file of the events of the day from the opening of the century to the present time. These series of newspapers proved of the greatest advantage to my work.

This expedition added to my library some 8,000 volumes. Three years later I made a second trip to Mexico, chiefly to verify certain statements and add a few points prior to closing the last volume of my *History of Mexico*. The railway being completed, the journey was nothing; and being brief and without special significance, I will inflict no further detail on the reader.

XXIX

TOWARD THE END

~

I HAD HOPED TO close my library to general work, and dismiss my assistants by January 1, 1887. I had yet several years of work to do myself, in any event, but I thought if I could get rid of the heavy library outlay of one or two thousand dollars a month, I should feel more inclined to take life easier, with less nervous haste and strain in my work.

Several causes combined to prevent this. As is usually the case, the completion of my history consumed more time than I had anticipated, the necessary rewriting and revision, not to mention numberless delays growing out of the cares and vicissitudes of business, being beyond calculation. The truth is, in looking back upon my life and its labors, I cannot but feel that I never have had a full and fair opportunity to do my best, to do as good work as I am capable of doing, certainly not as finished work as I might do with less of it and more time to devote to it, with fewer cares, fewer interruptions. I have often wondered what I might do were I not forced to "write history on horseback," as General Vallejo terms it. On the other hand, I have had much to be thankful for, and can only submit my work to the world for what it is worth.

During all my historical labors, particularly toward the latter part of the term, the necessity was more and more forced upon my mind, of some method whereby the men who had made this country what it is should receive fuller treatment. Thus, in writing

Chronicles of the Builders, here was an opportunity to do much better than simply present a collection of detached biographies. What would make it tenfold more interesting and valuable would be to take one each of these men of strength and influence, and after a thorough character study, place his portrait in artistic form and colors in the midst of the work which he has done, in company with kindred industries accomplished by others, and round the whole throw a frame-work of history.

During the earlier part of the long period the history was going into type, the movements of the family were regulated to a great extent by my youngest boy, Philip. Being naturally not very strong, and the penetrating winds driving him from San Francisco, we would visit the several springs and health districts of the coast as fancy or interest dictated, never being wholly out of reach of the printer.

I had long had in view a visit to Salt Lake City and the Colorado region, so that when, in August 1884, the boy began to cough in accents so familiar that there was no mistaking their significance, we picked him up—his mother and I—and planted ourselves with the whole family at the Continental hotel in the city of the saints, there remaining for six weeks.

There was much feeling existing at the time between the Mormons and the gentiles, the government being apparently in earnest in putting down polygamy, while the Mormons were just as determined to maintain the institution or die in the attempt. It was just upon the border, in point of time, of the long season of prosecution and persecution, of litigations and imprisonments which has not a parallel in the history of American morals.

We were not there, however, to take part in any controversy; we had come simply to gather facts, observe and study the social problem. I should probably have known long ere this how to answer the question, What is Mormonism? but I did not. Nor would there be entire unanimity among divines in answering the questions, What is Methodism? or Mohammedism? Very shallow ideas the world has in relation to the dogmas it fights and bleeds for.

Notwithstanding the large mass of material which had been sent to me, there were still gaps in my work that I wanted filled. There was little the Mormons would not do for us. John Taylor,[1] who was present and severely wounded at the assassination of Joseph Smith, was at the time president of the church, and Wilford Woodruff,[2] one of the twelve apostles, had charge of the historian's office. For these people had had an historian from the beginning of their existence as a religious sect. Mr Woodruff had an elaborately written journal in some twenty manuscript volumes, giving a history of the church and the doings of its members from the days of Nauvoo to date. Mr Woodruff gave up most of his time to me during this visit, among many others with whom I met.

While I was laboriously engaged in this office during most of my time in Salt Lake City, Mrs Bancroft saw many of the Mormon women, making their acquaintance, winning their friendship, and taking dictations from them. From Utah we went to Colorado, stopping at Cañon City, Leadville, Pueblo, Colorado Springs, and other points of historic interest and importance. We were everywhere received with the utmost cordiality. While my family were at Denver, enjoying the generous hospitality of the good people of the place, I spent a fortnight at Cheyenne, going through files of newspapers, and writing out the experiences of the prominent men.

Part of the winter of 1884-5 I spent in New Mexico, where I had interviews with most of the leading men, and obtained a large mass of material which was an absolute necessity to my work.

I cannot mention in this volume a hundredth part of the journeys made, the people seen, and the work done in connection with the labors of over a quarter of a century, collecting material and writing history, but enough has been presented to give the reader some faint conception of the time, labor, and money necessary for such an historical undertaking.

Referring once more to my method of writing history, which originated wholly with me, and grew out of the necessities of the case, I would remark on the general shyness of the wise men of the east at first to see any good in it, or ever admit that work so done could properly be placed in the category of history; then finally to see them come round, and not only acknowledge its advantages, and assert that it was the only feasible way to accomplish certain results, but to adopt the system themselves, apply it to important work, and give it out as of their own invention, or at least to take good care not to give the credit where it properly belonged.

The men of Harvard particularly, always slow to acknowledge the existence of any good thing outside of their own coterie, least of all to admit that a San Francisco bookseller could teach them how to write history, were puzzled how they might sometime apply this system to important work and send it forth as their own. Some ten years after the publication of my *Native Races*, there appeared in Boston what a prospectus called "History by a new method." It was not history, nor was the method new. It was by Justin Winsor, of the Harvard university library, and was called *Narrative and Critical History of America*, published 1884–9. Great stress is placed upon the method, which is called the "coöperative." That is to say, one man acting as editor, gives to twenty or fifty men each a topic on American history for him to write up, the intention being that all the topics given out shall be made to cover the entire range of American history.

"The magnitude of the undertaking," the prospectus goes on to say, "the dignity of the subject, and the acknowledged ability of the writers employed, give the work a strong claim upon public attention,...all overshadowed by the surpassing value of the method employed in its construction....We shall have less of speculation and theory, and more of verifiable facts. The temptation to warp the truth will be lessened by increased danger of detection." Further: "Individuals may philosophize on history in the future as they have in the past with excellent results, but the presentation of the facts, with a complete analysis and digest of the evidence collected, must be made by the coöperation of many minds."

This is indeed high praise of my method coming from such a source, and all the more significant not being intended,—all the more significant in coming from a quarter where this kind of work was not long since ridiculed as "machine-made history." Yet it is the same system as my own, though on a somewhat different plan.

Writing to me on September 21, 1886, A. W. Tourgée says: "I tried to get an article into an eastern magazine, on Coöperative Historical Work, comparing your system, which is homogenous and comprehensible, with Justin Winsor's hotch-pot, every mouthful of which is a surprise, but which leaves no uniformity of impression or coherence of thought; but I found the idea was sacrilegious in this latitude."

XXX

BURNED OUT!

≈

Mercury. "What's best for us to do then to get safe across?"
Charon. "I'll tell you. You must all strip before you get
in, and leave all those encumbrances on shore; and even
then the boat will scarce hold you all. And you take care,
Mercury, that no soul is admitted that is not in light
marching order, and who has not left all his encumbrances,
as I say, behind. Just stand at the gang-way and overhaul
them, and don't let them get in till they've stripped."

—Lucien

HERE WAS A pretty how-do-you-do! While I was buying
farms and building houses in San Diego, and dreaming of
a short period of repose on this earth before being called upon to
make once more an integral part of it, in the twinkling of an eye
I was struck down, as if by a thunderbolt from heaven.

For twenty years past I had been more than ordinarily interested in this southern extremity of the state, with its soft sunshine
and beautiful bay, the only break in the California coast-line
south of San Francisco that could be properly called a harbor,
and I had chipped in from time to time a few thousands for
lots and blocks, until satisfied that I had enough, when the great
commercial metropolis of the south should arise upon the spot,
to ruin all my children.

Drawing of the Walnut Creek farm and log cabin,
from the album *The Founding of a Family*,
courtesy of The Bancroft Library (BANC MSS 73/64 C. V.1)

Many times before this I had temporarily sought shelter for myself and family from the cold winds and fogs of San Francisco, often in the Napa country, and many times in the Ojai valley, and elsewhere. Then I wondered if there was not some place more accessible to my work, which would answer the purpose as well.

Ever since 1856 I had been gazing on the high hills back of Oakland and Berkeley, wondering what was on the other side; and one day I said I will go and see. So I mounted a horse, and wound round by San Pablo and through the hills until I came to Walnut creek, and beyond there to Ignacio valley, near the base of Monte Diablo, where I bought land, and planted it in trees and vines.

It was a broad and beautiful patch of earth, flat as possible, and covered with large scattering oaks, looking like many other parts of primeval California, only that the trees were larger, indicating unusual depth and strength of soil. The sun rises over the Devil's mountain, and the cool southwest wind comes over the high Oakland hills fresh from the ocean, the infrequent dry, hot, north winds alone taking advantage of the open country toward Martinez. It went against the grain to grub up the venerable oaks; but oak trees and fruit trees do not affiliate, and Bartlett pears are better than acorns, so all were cleared away except a group left for building sites and shelter of stock.[1]

For the most part it was a perfect climate, the heat of summer seldom being enervating, and but little frost in winter; but I was growing querulous over California airs, and said I wanted them quieter and softer than those which followed me even here, carrying their thick fog-banks to the summit of the highest westerly hills, and scattering them in finest mists filled with sunshine over the valleys below. So we took the train, my wife and I, and started south, stopping at Pasadena, Riverside, and elsewhere, all of which were too settled, too civilized for us. Then we came to San Diego, native enough for any one, the cobbley country around looking

Fruit crate label from H. H. Bancroft's Mt. Diablo Fruit Farm in Walnut Creek, with Paul Bancroft, Jr., in a field of flowers, courtesy of The Bancroft Library (BANC MSS 73/64 v.1:24)

H. H. Bancroft's Helix Farm in Spring Valley, outside of San Diego,
courtesy of the Spring Valley Historical Society

so dry and barren and forbidding that a week of exploration in
every direction was passed, setting out from our hotel in the early
morning and driving till night before we found a place in which
were seemingly united all the requisite possibilities. There we
were satisfied to rest, and then we made our purchase.

Spring valley it was called, from a large perpetual spring
nature had formed there; and it was the most attractive of any
spot within ten miles of the future metropolis. The nominal proprietor was Captain R. K. Porter, from whom I purchased land, a
tract of five hundred acres and more. The place I called the Helix
Farms, and entered in my book of life to spend my latter days
there.[2] I then returned north.

Keep at hard work too long an old horse and he becomes
worthless, but if care be taken to lighten his burdens as strength
and endurance fail, he will perform much good service during

his latter days. I was now reaching the period when I felt it absolutely necessary to turn myself out to grass or succumb entirely.

I was born on a farm; my earliest recollections were of farm life; my childhood home had been there, and if there were any rest and recuperation for me on earth I was sure it would be under like conditions. My work was nearly done. I had no further desire to mingle with the affairs of the world. I was content with what I had accomplished; or at least all I could do I had done, and I was sure that in no way could I better become young again than in spending much time with my little ones, in teaching them how to work and be useful, as my devoted parents had taught me.

It was on the 30th of April, 1886, that I was standing on the steps of the Florence hotel, at San Diego, when my wife drove up in her phaeton and handed me a telegram. "They said it was important," she remarked, and eyed me earnestly as I opened and read it. "What is it?" she asked. "Is it bad?" "About as bad as can be," I replied. It was from Mr N. J. Stone, manager of the History department of the business, and it read, "Store burning. Little hope of saving it." Half an hour later came another despatch, saying that nothing was saved but the account books.

The full effect of this calamity flashed through my brain on the instant: my beautiful building, its lofts filled to overflowing with costly merchandise, all gone, the results of thirty years of labor and economy, of headaches and heart-aches, eaten up by fire in an hour. The blow—though it felled me, seemed to strike softly, as if coming from a gloved hand, I was so powerless to oppose it. I was then building for my wife a summer residence overlooking the charming San Diego bay; but many days of sorrow and anguish were in store for me by reason of this infernal fire.

In this same hotel, seven months before, I had read of the Crocker fire, a similar catastrophe happening to a house of like business to ours. And I then thought, "this might as well have been

Burning of the Bancroft Building, 1886,
courtesy of The Bancroft Library (C-R 68 vol.5)

Bancroft." And now it was indeed Bancroft, and all their fine
establishment, the largest and finest in western America, swept
away in the midst of a desperate struggle to properly place my
histories upon the market. Twenty volumes had been issued, and
the firm was still $200,000 behind on the enterprise. But it was
gaining; the last month's business had been the most encouraging of all; when suddenly, office, stock, papers, correspondence,
printing-presses, type and plates, and the vast book-bindery, filled
with sheets and books in every stage of binding, were blotted
out, as if seized by Satan and hurled into the jaws of hell. There
was not a book left, not a volume of history saved; nine volumes
of history plates were destroyed, besides a dozen other volumes of
plates; two car loads of history paper had just come in, and 12,000

bound volumes were devoured by the flames. There was the enterprise left, and a dozen volumes of the history plates in the library basement, and that was all.

The loss thus in a moment, of over half a million of dollars, above all that any policies of insurance would cover, was not the worst of it. Our facilities for work were gone, machinery destroyed, and business connections suddenly snapped; at noon with one of the largest stocks in America, at night with nothing to sell!

I went down to the train, stowed myself away in a sleeper, and came to San Francisco, knowing I had to face the brunt of it, and endure the long-drawn agony of the catastrophe. My daughter was with me. Friends and sympathizers met me at Martinez. It was Sunday when I arrived and went to my city quarters. I kept my room until Tuesday; then pulled myself together and went down among the boys, who, poor fellows, were ready to cry when they saw me enter the miserable rooms on Geary street, to which they had been forced to fly with their books. I really felt more for them than for myself, as many of them had been dependent on the business for a livelihood for a quarter of a century, and they had wives and little ones to feed.

And my poor wife! I felt for her, from whom I was forced to part so abruptly. But most touching of all was the sympathy of the children. Paul said, "Papa shall have my chicken-money to help build his store," as he turned his face from his mother to hide his tears. At another time, looking at a new shot-gun, he said, "I am glad we have that gun, for now papa will not have to buy one." Little Philip would work all day and all night, and another bantling persisted in going about gathering nails in an old tin can for two days for his father. It is such testimonials as these that touch the strong man to the quick, and not the formal letters of sympathy and condolence that he gets.

It takes time to get accustomed to the new order of things. I wander about the city and note the many changes of late; I admire the new style of architecture, and note the lavish expenditure of the big bonanza men and others in the immediate vicinity of my still smoking ruins, and I feel sad to think that I have no longer a stake in this proud and wealthy city. For my ground must go. It is heavily mortgaged for money with which to print and publish my history. Seventeen years ago I gathered it up piece by piece, as I could get it, and pay for it, paying for one piece $6,000 and for one of like dimensions and equal value adjoining $12,000, thus buying seven lots in order to make up one of the size I wanted. And now it must all go into the capacious maw of some one not foolish enough to write and publish history.

It makes one's heart sore thus to walk about old familiar haunts and feel one's self a thing of the past. I am the ghost of a dead man stalking about the places formerly frequented while living.

Death is nothing, however. The wife and little ones, ah! there's the rub; all through my life of toil and self-abnegation I had looked forward to the proud position in which I might leave them, prouder by far than any secured by money alone, for I might easier have made ten millions than have collected this library and written this history. I must come down in my pretentions, however, there is no help for it.

For thirty years I have had a bookstore in this town, and the first and finest one here, or within two thousand miles of the place. Whenever I walked the streets, or met an acquaintance, or wanted money, or heard the bells ring for church, or drove into the park, or drew to my breast my child; whenever I went home at night, or down to business in the morning, or out to my library, or over to my farm, I had this bookstore. And now I have it not. It is I who should have been destroyed, and not this hive of industry which provided food for five hundred mouths.

For days and weeks I studiously avoided passing by the charred remains of my so lately proud establishment. I never liked looking on a corpse, and here was my own corpse, my own smouldering remains, my dead hopes and aspirations, all the fine plans and purposes of my life lying here a heap of ashes, and I could not bear to look upon them.

Half of the time during these days I was sick in bed with nervous prostration. Day after day and far into the night I lay there with an approximate statement of the condition of my finances in my hand, holding it before my eyes until I could not see the figures. It was the long and lingering suspense that piled up the agony; if I was to be hanged, and could know it at once, face it, and have it over, I could nerve myself for the emergency; but to keep myself nerved to meet whatever might come, not knowing what that would be, required all my fortitude and all my strength.

"What a blessing your library was not burned," the old-womanish men would say. "It was providential that you had moved it." Blessing! There was no blessing about it. Of a truth I should have felt relieved if the library had gone too, and so brought my illustrious career to a close. I felt with Shylock, as well take my history as take from me the means of completing my history. I could curse my fate; but with more show of reason, curse the management which, unknown to me, had crammed full to over-flowing eight large floors with precious merchandise in order to take advantage of low freights, at the same time cutting down the volume of insurance, so that when the match was applied in the basement of the furniture store adjoining, and a two-hours' blaze left only a heap of ashes, the old business would be killed.[3]

The business had not been very popular of late. It had many competitors and consequently many enemies; hence thousands were made happy by its fall. Yet some were kind enough to say that it was a public calamity; that there was nothing now in the country which might properly be called a bookstore, as compared with what ours was, and all that.

To be or not to be was the question. Should I make a struggle to recuperate my fortunes, or should I lay down my weary bones and drift as comfortably as I might into the regions of the unconscious? Were I to consider myself alone, had I no work to do affecting others, I could tell quickly what I would do. I would choose some sunny hillside and there follow with my eyes the rising and setting of the sun, until the evening should come when I might go down with it.

The question was not what I would like to do, but what I ought to do. I had never been accustomed to the easiest way, or to regard my pleasure as the first consideration in life. Except in moments of deepest depression, and then for only a moment, did I think of such a thing as giving up. I offered to give the remnant of the business to any one who would assume the responsibility, and save me the trouble and annoyance of cleaning it up; but no one would take it, and I was therefore compelled to do it myself.

I say there were other things than myself to be considered. There was the history, and the men engaged on it, and the pledges which had been made to the public and the subscribers. There was the business, and a large body of creditors that must be paid. There was my family, and all who should come after me; if I should fail myself and others now, who would ever after rise up and retrieve our fallen fortunes? Then, too, it was not in the power of man so constituted and so disciplined as I had been to sit down beside the business I had established in my boyhood, and labored to sustain and build up all throughout my life, and see the light of it go out, become utterly extinguished, making no effort to save it.

So I set about considering as coolly as I could the position of things, what might be done, what might not be done, and what it were best to try to do. It took two months to ascertain whether the business was solvent or not; for although most of the account-books had been saved, there were goods and invoices in transit, and new statements of accounts had to be obtained from every quarter.

Above all, it might be utterly beyond the question to continue the publication of the history. This would be indeed the greatest calamity that could befall. A half-finished work would be comparatively valueless; and not only would no one take up the broken threads and continue the several narratives, but there would be little hope of the work ever being again attempted by any one on the extensive and thorough plan I had marked out. It is true that much of the work that I had accomplished would be useful in the hands of another; the question was, however, would any government or individual undertake it?

I kept the old store lot because I could not sell it, buyers seeming to think it a special imposition if they could not profit by the fire. Finally, the savings banks sending me word that if I wanted to rebuild to come around and get the money, I saw in it a hundred thousand dollars better for me than any offer I could get for the lot. I determined to go on and rebuild, and at once started out to do so.

Then there was the library work to be considered. While comparatively speaking I was near the end, so near that I could begin to think of retiring to farm life, and a voyage of several years around the world as an educating expedition for my children, yet I had much to do, and this fire added a hundred fold to that, even should it be proved possible to complete the work at all. I had them make out for me at the library a schedule showing the exact condition of the work, what had been done, what remained to be done, what plates had been destroyed and what remained, and an estimate of the probable time and expense it would require to complete the history. Two years and twelve thousand dollars were the time and money estimated, but both time and money were nearly doubled before the end came.

It was interesting to observe the diverse attitudes assumed by different persons after the fire in the business and out of it. A singular phenomenon was a shoal of business sharks which sailed in around us, seeking something to devour. Best of all were the true and noble fellows of our own establishment, who stood by us regardless of any consequences to themselves. There is no higher or nobler work, no more pleasing sight, than to watch and assist the unfolding of true nobleness of character in young men of good impulses.

I noticed with pride that most of the heads of departments thus remaining had begun their business career with me and my historical work from first to last; and I swore to myself that if the business survived, these men should never regret their course, and I do not think they ever have. Nor should my assistants at the library be forgotten, several of whom, besides quite a number at the store, voluntarily cut down their salary in order to make as light as possible the burden of completing my work.

On the whole, we considered ourselves very fairly treated, both at the west and at the east, in the adjustment of difficulties arising from the fire. The insurance companies were entitled to every praise, paying their losses promptly before they were due. New friendships were made, and old friendships widened and cemented anew. I was specially gratified by the confidence moneyed men seemed to repose in me, granting me all the accommodations I desired, and thus enabling me quickly to recuperate my fortunes, as I will more fully narrate in the next and final chapter.

THE HISTORY
COMPANY AND THE
BANCROFT COMPANY

≫

*…the man who possesses real fortitude and magnanimity
will show it by the dignity of his behavior under losses,
and in the most adverse fortune.*
—Plutarch

As the goods arrived which were in transit at the time of the fire, they were put into a store in the Grand hotel, on Market street, of which we took a lease for a year. Orders came in and customers called, making their purchases, though in a limited way. Considering the crippled condition of the business and the general prostration of its affairs, the result was more favorable than might have been expected. In due time after the fire I was able to ascertain that the business was not only solvent, but had a margin of one hundred thousand dollars of resources above liabilities. To bring about this happy state of things, however, the utmost care and watchfulness, with the best of management were necessary.

A number of fragmentary concerns sprang up, thrown off from the parent institution in the whirl of the great convulsion. Our law department was united with the business of Sumner Whitney, and a large and successful law-book publishing house was thus established under the able management of good men from both houses. The history department was segregated from the old business, and reorganized and incorporated under the name of The History Company.

All through the whole of it the main question, and the only question, was, could the publishing business pay its debts? When I ascertained that the old business was solvent, and would pay its debts without the further sacrifice of my resources, I wrote my wife, who was still in San Diego attending to affairs there, that she need have no fear of the future, for if I lived we would yet have enough and to spare.

Buying an additional lot, so as to make a width of one hundred feet on Stevenson street, having still seventy-five feet frontage on Market street, in something over a year I had completed on the old site a strong and beautiful edifice, a feature of Market street, and of the city, which I called The History Building. Its architecture was original and artistic, the structure monumental, and it was so named in consideration of my historical efforts.

I had seen from the first that it would be necessary as soon as possible to secure some steady income, both at San Diego and San Francisco. In the former place, property was so rapidly increasing in value, with increased taxation and street assessments, that unless it could be made productive a portion of it would have to be sold. Some of it, the outside lands, were sold, and with the proceeds, and what I could scrape together in San Francisco, we managed to erect a business building there, which brought in good returns. Then there was the ground-rent from a hundred lots or so, which helped materially. No money which I had ever handled gave me half the pleasure as that which I was able to send to my wife at this time; for although it lessened and made more difficult my chances of success in San Francisco, it removed my family further every day from possible want, and thus gave me renewed strength for the battle.

The History Building, 1890s,
now the Bancroft Building, at 721 Market Street,
courtesy of The Bancroft Library (BANC MSS 73/64 vol. 1)

Up to this time the publication and sale of my historical series
had been conducted as one of the departments of the general
business, under the management of Nathan J. Stone. As this
business had assumed large proportions, sometimes interfering

with the other departments, not always being in harmony with them or with the general management, it was finally thought best to organize an independent company, having for its object primarily the publications of my books, together with general book-publishing, and acting at the same time as an agency for strictly first-class eastern subscription publications.

It may be not out of place to give here some account of the manner in which the publication and sale of this historical series was conducted; for if there had been anything unusual in gathering the material and writing these histories, the method by which they were published and placed in the hands of readers was no less remarkable.

Ordinarily, for a commercial man formally to announce to the world that he was about to write and publish a series of several histories, which would number in all thirty-nine volumes, would be regarded as a somewhat visionary proposition. Still further out of the way would it seem for the publishers of the series to bring forward a prospectus and invite subscriptions beforehand for the whole thirty-nine volumes at once. We did not know that the publication and sale could be successfully effected on this basis, but we determined to try.

First, to place this work before men of discrimination and taste so as to make them understand it, its inception and execution, required men of no common ability, and such men must receive adequate compensation for superior intelligence and energy. Secondly, when once the patron should understand the nature and scope of the work, if he desire any of it, he would want it all. Thirdly, considering the outlay of time and money on each section, a subscription to only one volume, or one set of volumes, would in no way compensate the publisher. Throughout the series are constant cross-references, by which repetitions, otherwise necessary for the proper understanding of each several part, are saved, thus making the history of Mexico of value to California and *vice versa*.

Therefore, if ever the work should be placed before the public for sale, it should be done so as to command and retain for it the respect and approbation of the best men. In due time fortune directed to the publishers the man of all others best fitted to the task.

Nathan Jonas Stone was born in New Hampshire in 1843. In 1863, Mr Stone came to California by way of Panamá, arriving with just ten cents in his pocket. He spent several years acting as teacher and deputy superintendent of an industrial school farm. In 1867, he entered the house of H. H. Bancroft, acting as manager first of the subscription department. In 1872, he became interested in the awakening of civilization in Japan and opened his own business in Yokohama. Obliged by ill-health to abandon business, he returned to San Francisco in 1878, and eventually accepted the important responsibility of assuming the general management of the histories' publication and sale. No one could have been better fitted for this arduous task than he. With native ability were united broad experience and a keen insight into men and things. And with unflinching faith and loyalty, Mr Stone stood by the proposition until was wrought out of it the most complete success.

A S THE HISTORY BUILDING drew near completion, the proposition arose to move the business back into its old quarters; but it had become so crippled in its resources and reduced in its condition, that I did not feel like assuming the labor, risk, and responsibility of the necessary increased expenses.

I had long been anxious to get out of business rather than go deeper into it. I did not care for the money should it succeed; I wanted nothing further now than to get myself away from everything of the kind. Yet there was my old business which I had established in my boyhood, and worked out day by day and year by year into magnificent and successful proportions; for there had never been a year since its foundation that it had not grown and flourished. Through good and evil times it had stood bravely by me, by my family, my history, my associates, and employés, and I could not desert it now. I could not see it die or go to the dogs without an effort to save it. The country was rapidly going forward. There must soon be a first-class bookstore in San Francisco. There was none such now, and if ours did not step to the front and assume that position, some other one would. Immediately after the fire the remarks were common, "It is a public loss"; "We have nowhere, now, to go for our books"; "Your store was not appreciated until it was gone."

My family were now all well provided for, through the rise of real estate in San Diego. What I had besides need not affect them one way or the other.

So I laid my plans accordingly, and in company with W. B. Bancroft, Mr Colley, and Mr Dorland, all formerly connected with the original house of H. H. Bancroft and Company, I organized and incorporated The Bancroft Company, and moved the old business back upon the old site, but into new and elegant quarters. Behold the new creation! Once more we had a bookstore, one second to none in all this western world—an establishment which was a daily pride and pleasure, not so widely spread as the old one, but in many respects better conditioned. Above all, we were determined to popularize it, and place it upon a higher plane than ever it had before enjoyed. And we succeeded.

The management of The Bancroft Company was placed in the hands of my nephew, W. B. Bancroft, who had been well instructed in the business, and had ever been loyal to it. At the time of the fire he was at the head of the manufactory, having under him two or three hundred men. Husbanding his influence and resources, he started a printing office on his own account, and was on the broad road to success when he was invited to unite his manufactory with the old business under the new name, and assume the management, which he finally consented to do. Thus he, with the others, passed through the fiery furnace unscathed, and with them deserved the success which he achieved.

Thus, with fresh blood, good brains, and ample capital, there was no reason apparent why the new business should not in time far outstrip the old, and on its centennial in 1956 stand unapproached by any similar institution in the new and grandest of empires on the shores of the Pacific.

THE END

AFTERWORD

Charles B. Faulhaber

*L*ITERARY INDUSTRIES IS a personal autobiography, but it is also, as its title indicates, very much the account of the creation of Hubert Howe Bancroft's two enduring legacies, The Bancroft Library and *Bancroft's Works*. They represent, respectively, the ingathering and preservation of historical documents and the subsequent use and publication of those documents.

For students and scholars at the end of the nineteenth century, *Bancroft's Works* offered a comprehensive historical account of the exploration, conquest, and development of the North American West. While still important as a sourcebook, it has long since ceded its place of honor as the definitive history of California to later works, most notably Kevin Starr's California Dream series.

While *Bancroft's Works* are today known primarily to advanced students of California history, The Bancroft Library at the University of California, Berkeley, remains Bancroft's signal achievement. Begun, as *Literary Histories* records, simply as a reference collection for the compilation of the *Hand-book Almanac for the Pacific States* (1862), by the latter part of the 1860s it had become an all-consuming passion. Bancroft, in describing his collecting activities, says, "I did not stop to consider, I did not care, whether the book was of any value or not; it was easier and cheaper to buy it than to spend time in examining its value. The most worthless trash may prove some fact wherein the best book is deficient, and this makes the trash valuable."

Professor Henry Morse Stephens, perhaps the person most responsible for the University of California's acquisition of The Bancroft Library, described, in 1906, H. H.'s efforts as follows:

> Mr. Bancroft's greatest characteristic as a collector was that he had imagination. He swept in with his dragnet all sorts of stuff—business directories, diaries, handbills, account books. He had the imagination even to see the importance of ships' logs, and he took these in. He sent a man to Alaska for all the records of the early fur companies. As a result we have more of these than there are at St. Petersburg....One knows not where to begin or end an enumeration. There are five thousand volumes of newspapers, many of them country newspapers at that, many of which exist alone in this collection. There is a magnificent pile of briefs in Spanish land cases; an extraordinary collection of records of the old Missions. We can trace the pious Father Serra, founder of missions, step by step on his journeys. We have also the entire records of the old Presidio in San Francisco; large masses of correspondence of old Spanish families; the actual minutes of the Vigilance Committees, which are under lock and key and not to be opened until all the participants have passed away. ("Address before the California Library Association: The Bancroft Library," Henry M. Stephens Papers, BANC MSS CB 926, carton 2).

In 1881, fearful that another San Francisco fire would destroy the library, H. H. moved it from the Bancroft Building at 721 Market Street (which was in fact destroyed by fire in 1886), to a fire-proof building constructed specifically for the library on Valencia Street. There it survived the 1906 earthquake and fire; two weeks later it was moved to Berkeley, having been acquired by the University the previous fall.

This was one of the signal events that led to Berkeley's current eminence as one of the world's most distinguished public universities. As University of California President Benjamin Ide Wheeler stated:

> The purchase of The Bancroft Library marks a great day in the history of the University....It means the inevitable establishment at Berkeley of the center for future research in the history of Western America; it means the creation of a school of historical study at the University of California; it means the emergence of the real University of study and research out of the midst of the Colleges of elementary teaching and training.

Despite Wheeler's celebratory comments, the Regents of the University were not disposed to invest many resources in their new acquisition; the annual budget for 1906–1907 was $900, mostly for salaries, nothing for new acquisitions. Stephens was placed in charge of the library and almost immediately organized the Academy of Pacific Coast History among wealthy San Franciscans, including Phoebe Apperson Hearst, James K. Moffitt, and Sigmund Stern. However, perhaps Stephens's most important action for the Library's future was the recruitment of Herbert Eugene Bolton of Stanford as professor of Latin American history. Named curator of The Bancroft in 1916, Bolton became its first formal director in 1920, after Stephens's death.

Under Bolton and his students Herbert I. Priestley (1940–1944) and George P. Hammond (1946–1965), The Bancroft Library continued to focus on the North American West in the broadest sense, expanding its holdings, particularly in materials relating to northern Mexico and the American Southwest, Bolton's Borderlands. A succession of curators, distinguished scholars in their own right, helped to implement that expansion: Frederick J. Teggart, Charles Chapman, Jacob Bowman, Dale Morgan, and J. S. Holliday. As a result, The Bancroft became the world's preeminent repository for serious research in the field.

There the collection areas stood until the 1960s, but almost twenty years into Hammond's tenure he began to expand The Bancroft anew. The University Archives and the Regional Oral History Office (ROHO) were gathered under the Library's wing in 1963 and 1965, respectively, continuing the focus on California history. Most dramatically, under James D. Hart (1970–1990), Hammond's successor and my predecessor, in 1970 The Bancroft assumed responsibility for all of the University Library's rare books and special collections, from ancient Egyptian papyri to the Mark Twain Papers, and, in 1972, established the History of Science and Technology Program.

At the end of the twentieth century, The Bancroft was still following its founder's example. Just as H. H. had used the latest information technology—the steam-powered printing press—for the dissemination of his works, so, too, has The Bancroft Library pioneered, using advances in digital technology to make its treasures accessible all over the world to scholars who could not come to Berkeley. In the late 1980s The Bancroft became the first special collections library in the world to put its catalog online. Almost overnight, usage doubled.

Finally, just as H. H. constructed a new building to protect his collections, so have the library's supporters. With the Doe Library Annex—The Bancroft Library's home—rated "poor" seismically, the building was gutted to the bare walls and floors between 2005 and 2008, seismically strengthened, and reconfigured both to protect the library and to make it more usable for staff and patrons. The state of California provided funds for the seismic work, but everything else was paid for by private donors.

Over the last thirty years a succession of brilliant staff members have continued to build The Bancroft Library's collections: Elizabeth Gudde, Patricia Howard, Walter Brem, and Theresa Salazar for Western Americana and Latin Americana; Larry Dinnean and Jack von Euw for the Pictorial Collections; Jim Kantor,

Bill Roberts, and David Farrell for University Archives; Tony Bliss for rare books and literary manuscripts; Bob Hearst for the Mark Twain Papers; Willa Baum and Richard Cándida-Smith for ROHO; a constant presence over the last forty years, the omnicompetent Peter Hanff, Deputy Director; and watching over all with a passionate eye, my successor, Elaine Tennant, Professor of German.

NOTES

II

1. Charles Nordhoff (1830–1901) was a journalist who wrote for many East Coast publications.

2. Sara Jane Lippincott (1823–1904) went by the pseudonym Grace Greenwood as a writer. In her journalism and lectures she advocated for abolition and women's rights in particular, along with writing poetry and children's books.

3. Englishman Walter M. Fisher (1849–1919) wrote an early social commentary on California based on his four-year stay there in the early 1870s, a book called *The Californians* (London: Macmillan, 1876).

4. Oscar Wilde (1854–1900) traveled to California in 1882 on a tour of the United States that lasted over a year.

III

1. P. G. Hamerton (1834–1894) was an English artist and writer. The quotation is from *The Intellectual Life* (Boston: Roberts Brothers, 1873).

2. Edward Bulwer-Lytton (1803–1873) was a baron, a politician, and a well-received writer in England. His novels provided several enduring literary lines, including "the pen is mightier than the sword." *Caxtoniana* is subtitled *A Series of Essays on Life, Literature, and Manners* (Leipzig: Bernhard Tauchnitz, 1864).

IV

1. Founded in 1831, the Granville Literary and Theological Institute changed its name to Dennison University in 1853 after a benefactor.

2. Park Benjamin, Sr. (1809–1864) was a poet, journalist, and newspaper editor well known in his time, especially as a result of his lecture circuit in New England. The British writer G. P. R. James (1799–1860) served as consul in the United States. He lived in New England and Virginia in the 1850s. Gough probably refers to John B. Gough (1817–1886), whose eloquence about his alcoholism and recovery made him a famed temperance speaker in New England and his native England.

3. George L. Kenny (1823–1902) came from Ireland to the United States in the 1840s and found work at George Derby's bookshop in Buffalo. He became Bancroft's brother-in-law after Kenny's first wife died and he married Bancroft's widowed sister Cecilia Bancroft Derby. George and Cecilia married in 1868. He died in Los Angeles. For more, see "My First Forty Years in California Politics, 1922–1962," an oral history of George L. Kenny's grandson, Robert W. Kenny, University of California, Los Angeles.

V

1. Peter Smith was a doctor who attended to San Francisco's poor from 1849 to 1854. When he sought repayment for his services from the city, an imbroglio ensued involving fraudulent land titles portioned out by the city as repayment for services rendered in the 1850s. Many of these lots were actually "water lots" in Mission Bay, not yet filled in, but sold vigorously in a spate of specious speculation.

2. Self-appointed law keepers organized this early Vigilance Committee on June 9, 1851, and promptly hanged a man on June 10 for stealing. Three others were later hanged, one whipped, and two dozen either deported or forced to leave California before the committee, grown to seven hundred men, disbanded in September. A second Vigilance Committee reemerged in 1856.

3. Eliza Biscaccianti (1824–1896) was originally from Boston and became a star opera singer in San Francisco in the 1850s. With little formal

entertainment available at the time, such concerts were very popular with the middle and upper classes of San Francisco.

4. Anti-Chinese sentiments against the so-called "Yellow Peril" were flamed by the influx of Chinese citizens escaping both a series of wars, including the British-Chinese Opium Wars, and the dissolution of civil society in China. They were also lured by advertised opportunities to work in what was called "Gold Mountain," or California. Later efforts to restrict Chinese access to land and work escalated to the nation's first anti-immigrant law, the Chinese Exclusion Act of 1882.

5. In the 1830s, that plaza sat at the center of the village called Yerba Buena under Mexican rule. The plaza was later renamed Portsmouth Square under the Americans.

6. Bancroft references various places in the foothills of the Sierra where he and his father and brother worked and traveled, including Long Bar on the Yuba River, Rich Bar and Indian Bar on the Feather River, and Browns Valley, east of Marysville.

7. The Rassette House, at the corner of Bush and Sansome, was one of San Francisco's earliest hotels. A five-story wood-framed building that housed up to 416 guests, it fell victim to fire, like many other of San Francisco's early structures, in May of 1853.

VI

1. At 721 Market Street is the current site of the Bancroft Building, now a collection of commercial offices, whose façade is designated as a historical landmark.

2. Bancroft put his business in his brother's name, calling it "A. L. Bancroft & Co." after his younger brother Albert Little (1841–1914). For many years, A. L. was instrumental in helping H. H. manage his printing and publishing enterprises.

3. A devastating drought from 1862 to 1865 decimated cattle herds and had other impacts on the agricultural industry. The opening of the First Transcontinental Railroad, in 1869, was expected to create new markets for California's goods. In fact, the new transportation made eastern

goods much cheaper to purchase directly, thus creating a challenge for California merchants, forcing many to go out of business, as Bancroft notes.

VII

1. Many of the original materials relating to Bancroft's collecting process and the writing of his histories can be found at The Bancroft Library under the name of Records of the Library and Publishing Company, 1864–1910, BANC MSS B-C 7.

IX

1. A leader from the early days of the Latter-day Saints, Brigham Young (1801–1877) helped found Salt Lake City, served as governor of Utah Territory, and was president of his church from 1847 until his death.

XI

1. John Swett arrived in California in 1853 to mine gold but quickly turned to teaching. He became the state's Superintendent of Education in 1863 and later held other leadership roles in the San Francisco education arena.

2. In the original version of this volume, Bancroft provides much more detail about these assistants, as well as acknowledgment of the contributions of many others in his workshop, including: Walter M. Fisher, T. Arundel Harcourt, J. J. Peatfield, Alfred Bates, Alfred Kemp, Edward P. Newkirk, Thomas Matthew Copperthwaite, Ivan Petroff, Charles Welch, Amos Bowman, Rosendo V. Corona, Emilio Piña, Labadie, Manuel Fernandez Martinez, and Martin Barientos.

XII

1. Jean Paul Richter (1763–1825) was a German writer known for his Romantic-era stories and novels.

XIII

1. H. H. Bancroft published Franklin Tuthill's history in 1866.

2. Daniel C. Gilman (1831–1908) graduated with a degree in geography from Yale, where he subsequently worked as a librarian. He served as the president of the University of California from 1872 to 1875 and then returned east to become the first president of Johns Hopkins University.

XIV

1. Francis Parkman (1823–1893) was a horticulturalist and historian who wrote a history of the early Oregon Trail, as well as an important work on the roles of France and England in the United States.

2. Charles Francis Adams, Sr. (1807–1886) was a lawyer, politician, and writer. Son of President John Quincy Adams, he built the first presidential library to honor his father's work.

3. James Russell Lowell (1819–1891) was a significant figure among the intellectuals of the 1850s and beyond. A New England poet of the American Romantic period, a professor at Harvard, and an editor of the *Atlantic Monthly*, Lowell also served as a diplomat and critic.

4. Henry Wadsworth Longfellow (1807–1882), poet, translator, and Harvard professor, became highly popular during his time for his lyrical poetry based on legend and myth.

5. Wendell Phillips (1811–1884) was an ardent voice for liberation and equality in many movements of his time, including abolition, women's rights, labor, and Native American citizenship.

6. John Greenleaf Whittier (1807–1892), a Quaker and poet, spoke out in favor of abolition as a writer and editor.

7. Ralph Waldo Emerson (1803–1882) played a central role in the Transcendentalist movement among mid-nineteenth-century American writers and philosophers, writing and lecturing widely.

8. Frederick A. P. Barnard (1809–1889) was a scientist and educator, teaching in many disciplines, including literature, mathematics, philosophy, chemistry, and astronomy. Barnard College was named in his honor.

9. William Dean Howells (1837–1920) was a writer, literary critic, and the editor of the *Atlantic Monthly*.

10. Oliver Wendell Holmes, Sr. (1809–1894) was another of the renowned New England poets of his time. He was also a physician, professor, essayist, and lecturer.

11. Devoted to various causes for equal rights, T. W. Higginson (1822–1913) was a famed abolitionist, Civil War colonel, and Unitarian minister.

12. Bancroft devoted thirty-five pages to the scholars and writers he met and the discussions that ensued, here considerably shortened.

13. Some modern-day sleuthing by Dr. Charles Faulhaber discovered a familial link between H. H. Bancroft and George Bancroft (1800–1891). Hubert's great-great-grandfather was one Lt. Samuel Bancroft of Granville, Massachusetts. Samuel begat Azariah, who begat Azariah Ashley, who begat Hubert. Samuel Bancroft also begat Aaron Bancroft who was George Bancroft's father, making Hubert the first cousin, once removed, of George. The link was discovered on Family Tree Maker; see the family tree of Christine Van Epps created by Linda Santiago on Geneology.com for the descendants of William Bancroft, 1500.

14. He is probably referring to Henry Draper (1837–1882), a physician, astronomer, and one of the first to practice astrophotography.

15. Mark Twain (1835–1910) gained fame by writing humorously about life at the margins of society, including California during the gold rush and later. Happily for the inheritors of The Bancroft Library, now at the University of California at Berkeley, Twain's private papers are also lodged there.

16. Charles D. Warner (1829–1900), Twain's close friend and literary collaborator, was a novelist and essayist in his own right, often speaking up in defense of contributions to the public good, such as park development.

17. Bancroft kept scrapbooks of the collected reviews of *Native Races* and other clippings, now located at The Bancroft Library. See Notices and Reviews of the Library and of the *Native Races of the Pacific States*: Clippings dated from 1869–1877, scrapbook, 3 volumes, xfE13.B21.B2.

XV

1. As Bancroft notes, Mariano Guadalupe Vallejo (1807–1890) was the last of the military leaders of California. His military actions included managing shifting alliances and conflicts between California's indigenous peoples and embattled Mexican factions, and the invading Americans. During the Bear Flag Revolt of June 1846, Vallejo was taken prisoner but facilitated a peaceful acceptance of the new American government. He suffered huge losses of land and money in the legal battles to keep his property in the transition to American rule.

XVII

1. Juan Bautista Alvarado (1808–1882) became governor at age twenty-seven during a time of increasing tensions within the Mexican government and with the Americans. Alvarado's mother was a Vallejo, and he grew up with Mariano Vallejo in Monterey.

2. This chapter, originally entitled "Alvarado and Castro," also concerns efforts to gain the papers of Manuel Castro. Castro (1821–1891) was a captain in the Mexican army of California during the years of the U.S. incursion; he fiercely defended his country in several battles. When the Californios were routed, Castro fled to Mexico but returned in 1852. Offended by the expropriation of his country's territory, Castro never claimed U.S. citizenship. He later was nominally given the rank of general.

XVIII

1. William E. P. Hartnell (1798–1854) arrived in Monterey in 1822 to participate in trade and ranching, but ended up opening a preparatory school. Vallejo and Alvarado were among his students.

2. Thomas O. Larkin (1802–1858) appeared in Mexican California in 1832 as a trader and clerk. He played an increasingly important role in negotiating between the Californios, whom he had befriended since his arrival, and the Americans, an effort that culminated in his becoming U.S. consul to the short-lived California Republic following the Bear Flag Revolt and transition to American government.

XIX

1. A complex man, John C. Frémont (1813–1890) played roles as explorer, military leader, and political aspirant. He was married to Jessie Benton, daughter of Senator Thomas Hart Benton from Missouri, a proponent of Manifest Destiny and the expansion of the United States to the then distant western shore. Frémont was instrumental in the 1846 Bear Flag Revolt, in which early American settlers attempted to claim California territory for the United States. As Frémont's reputation was tarnished over time, he saw in H. H. Bancroft's histories a means for setting the record straight—to his benefit.

2. Major John Wesley Powell (1834–1902) was a significant geological explorer of the West, following on his career as a U.S. soldier in the Civil War, in which he lost his right arm. Nonetheless, he undertook many challenging explorations, including a three-month trip down the Colorado River, making him the first to chart the Grand Canyon.

3. Judge Stephen Field (1816–1899) came West in 1848 from New York and set up a legal practice in Marysville in the rough and tumble days when punishment included the whipping post. Eventually Field became California's chief justice (1859–1863), replacing David Terry, who left the state after killing California state senator David Broderick in a duel.

4. Bancroft probably refers to Ainsworth R. Spofford (1825–1908), a journalist, publisher, and later librarian of the U.S. Congress (1864–1897).

5. Brantz Mayer (1809–1879) was an author, lawyer, and founder of the Maryland Historical Society.

6. Johann A. Sutter (1803–1880) was a Swiss citizen who arrived in San Francisco in 1839, then made his way to Sacramento, where he built a fort to supply incoming pioneers based on a land grant made by then governor Alvarado. At his mill on the American River at Coloma, gold was found by his employee John Marshall in early 1848.

7. Pio Pico (1801–1894) was twice the governor of Alta California, including the last to serve when the Americans won the territory.

8. Romualdo Pacheco (1831–1899) was a Californio politician. He served in the California State Senate, in the U.S. House of Representatives, and as the state's twelfth governor, from February to December of 1875.

9. José María Iglesias (1823–1891) was a journalist, lawyer, politician, and jurist. As president of the Supreme Court, he declared the presidency of Sebastian Lerdo illegitimate, and he was next in line to serve as interim president of Mexico from October 1876 to January 1877. His presidency in turn was challenged by Lerdo, so along with several of his supporters, including Prieto and Palacio, Iglesias fled Mexico.

XX

1. Edwin M. Stanton (1814–1869), a lawyer, was sent to California in 1858 by the U.S. Attorney General to investigate a conspiracy to defraud the U.S. government of vast land claims. He later served as secretary of war under Lincoln.

2. The original Spanish and Mexican California Archives records were kept in the U.S. Surveyor General's Office in San Francisco. H. H. Bancroft had Thomas Savage direct the copying of the 273 volumes and loose papers from 1876 to 1877. The originals, later stored at San Francisco City Hall, were destroyed in the 1906 earthquake and fire. A few burned remnants of the originals are housed in the National Archives. These documents would have been completely lost without Bancroft's intervention.

XXI

1. Junipero Serra (1713–1784) and Fermín Lasuen (1736–1803) were Franciscan fathers who helped found and develop the chain of missions along Alta California.

2. Juan Bandini (1800–1859) arrived in San Diego in 1834 and became involved in commerce. His daughter Arcadia Bandini de Stearns Baker (1825–1912) married Abel Stearns at age fourteen and reigned over Los Angeles society. Stearns (1798–1871) came to Los Angeles in 1829 and became a significant cattle rancher and landowner, and later a state politician.

3. Born in San Diego, Andrés Pico (1810–1876) had a distinguished career in the military under Mexican rule, was governor of Alta California, served in the state government under American rule, and had much success in ranching.

4. Ygnacio Sepúlveda (1842–1916) was a lawyer who served in the California legislature and then as a county and district judge, finally becoming one of the first Superior Court judges for Los Angeles, in 1879.

5. Robert M. Widney (1838–1929) arrived in California in 1857. He became a lawyer, judge, and founder of the University of Santa Clara.

6. Mission San Buenaventura lists Rev. John Comapla as the "Spiritual Shepherd" of the church from 1861 to 1877. The mission was founded by Junipero Serra on March 31, 1782.

7. Alexander S. Taylor (1817–1876) arrived in California in 1848. He was a collector and writer, most notably the author of a column called "Indianology of California" for the magazine *California Farmer and Journal of Useful Arts.*

8. José M. Amador (1781–1883) had been a soldier and later was granted ranch lands, all of which he lost when such Mexican land grants were not honored by the new American government.

9. Manuel Requena (1802–1876) was a local leader in Los Angeles government under both the Mexicans and the Americans.

XXII

1. Sir James Douglas (1803–1877) arrived in Canada as a fur trader and later served as governor of Vancouver Island from 1851 to 1864 and of British Columbia from 1858 to 1864.

2. James G. Swan (1818–1900) served as an Indian agent in Washington state and wrote ethnographies of the Makah Indian people.

3. An immigrant from England, John Minto (1822–1915) arrived in Oregon in 1844. His career included sheep ranching and serving four terms in the state legislature.

4. Matthew Deady (1824–1893) worked as a blacksmith while attending school to become a teacher and lawyer. He moved to the Oregon Territory in 1849 with the army. Eventually Deady served in the legislature and as a judge, including on the Oregon Supreme Court.

5. William Strong (1817–1887) gained his law degree from Yale and moved to the Oregon Territory in 1850. He eventually served as a Supreme Court justice for both Oregon and Washington states.

XXIII

1. The original reference notes that Bancroft had pasted on sheets of Manila paper can be found at The Bancroft Library under Bancroft Reference Notes, BANC MSS B-C 1 through BANC MSS B-M 2.

2. Suspected to have mastered the magic of alchemy, Albertus Magnus (c. 1206–1290) was a German Catholic scholar of religion, philosophy, and science.

XXV

1. Orson Pratt (1811–1881) was an elder in the early Mormon church as of 1831. He joined Brigham Young's initial pioneer group on the migration from Missouri to Utah, arriving to settle in the Salt Lake Valley in July 1847.

2. Joseph Smith (1805–1844), in the very few years of his life, was the founder of the Church of Jesus Christ of Latter-day Saints. He initiated thousands into his faith, which was based on teachings in the Book of Mormon, which he supposedly translated from ancient plates. He led his followers to Ohio, Missouri, and Illinois before his life was cut short in a dramatic mob action.

XXVII

1. Henry Oak did work very hard for his employer, and soon after he communicated his exhaustion to Bancroft, Oak quit the firm. In later years, he became embittered about the work he had done for H. H. Bancroft, feeling that he had not been properly acknowledged. In the controversy over Bancroft's use of writing assistants, Oak contributed his own critique in a long essay called *"Literary Industries" in a New Light* (San Francisco: Bacon Printing Company, 1893).

XXVIII

1. Ygnacio M. Altamirano (1834–1893) was a journalist, teacher, critic, and politician. A prolific writer, he authored poetry, essays, fiction, and biography.

2. Alfredo Chavero (1841–1906) was a Mexican renaissance man: poet, historian, playwright, lawyer, archeologist, and politician.

3. Ireneo Paz (1836–1924) was a lawyer, journalist, and writer of history.

4. Formerly a general in the Mexican military, Porfirio Diaz (1830–1915) served as president of Mexico from 1876 to 1911, minus a brief interim presidency served by Manuel Gonzalez. Dedicated to progressive reforms, his rule eventually became dictatorial and led to the armed struggle of the Mexican Revolution (1910–1920 or so), which ousted him from power.

5. Manuel Gonzalez (1833–1893) was a military man who played an important role combatting the French intervention. He served as president of Mexico from 1880 to 1884, hand-picked by his friend and predecessor Porfirio Diaz, who was attempting to maintain his control over the country while technically out of office.

XXIX

1. John Taylor (1808–1887), an Englishman, was converted to Mormonism by his wife, and later became a preacher and church elder. He was imprisoned with Smith when the mob attacked, and was severely wounded himself. He later settled in the Salt Lake Valley with Brigham Young.

2. Wilford Woodruff (1807–1898) was the fourth president of the Church of Jesus Christ of Latter-day Saints, from 1889 until his death. He had an important role in ending the practice of plural marriage, in 1890.

XXX

1. Bancroft named his farm the Mt. Diablo Fruit Farm. His son Philip inherited the property, and he in turn passed it along to his son, Philip, Jr. The wife of Philip, Jr., Ruth Petersson Bancroft, developed forty acres of the farm into a now world-renowed succulent garden, called the Ruth Bancroft Garden, which, when the farm property was sold in the 1970s, has since been surrounded by the suburban homes of Walnut Creek.

2. As Bancroft notes, the family developed the Spring Valley property as a farm, growing olives, citrus, and other crops. The family owned Helix Farm for many years, with son Griffing later managing it. The land was sold not long after H. H. Bancroft's death, in 1918. A few of the original buildings remain as the seat of the Spring Valley Historical Society and the Bancroft Ranch House Museum.

3. Bancroft's brother, Albert Little (A. L.) was in charge of the whole enterprise. His failure to insure adequately the building and its contents became the source of a bitter falling out between the two brothers. H. H. reputedly never spoke to his brother again, and he even excised all references to A. L. by name from his autobiography.

BIBLIOGRAPHY

B ELOW ARE LISTED the specific shelfmarks of photographs and documents mentioned in *Literary Industries*. All are located in The Bancroft Library unless otherwise noted.

FAMILY PHOTOGRAPHS

Bancroft, Matilda G. *Founding of a Family*. Album of photos and miscellany. BANC MSS 73/64 C. V.1.

Palmer Family Album. Photo of Curtis Howe, H. H. Bancroft's maternal grandfather. BANC PIC 1990.035 ALB.

OTHER ITEMS

Amador, José. *Memorias sobre la historia de California*. Dictation recorded by Thomas Savage for The Bancroft Library. 1877. BANC MSS C-D 28.

Anderson, Alexander C. *History of the Northwest Coast*. Victoria, British Columbia, 1878. BANC MSS P-C 2.

Andrade, D. J. M. *Catalogue de la Riche Bibliotèque de D. José María Andrade*. XZ1431.A55.

Bancroft, Hubert H. *Life of Robert M. Widney, 1888–1891*. BANC MSS C-D 782.

———. Notices and Reviews of the Library and of the *Native Races of the Pacific States*. Scrapbook of clippings dated from 1869 to 1877, 3 volumes. xfE13.B21.B2.

———. Records of the Library and Publishing Company, 1864–1910. BANC MSS B-C 7. (Note: The guide to this collection helps in searching for much of the correspondence mentioned in *Literary Industries,* including that of Enrique "Henry" Cerruti, Henry Oak, and Mariano G. Vallejo.)

Bancroft, Kate. Journal, Bancroft Family Correspondence. UC San Diego, Mandeville Special Collections Library. MSS 0039.

Bancroft, Matilda Griffing. Diary. 1876. BANC MSS 83/22c.

Bandini, Juan. Family papers, *Documentos para la historia de California, 1776–1850.* BANC MSS C-B 68-69.

Cerruti, Henry (Enrique). *Ramblings in California,* 2 vols. BANC MSS C-E 115.

Chadwick, Stephen F. Dictation. Oregon, 1887. BANC MSS P-A 142:23.

Clarke, Harriet T. *A Young Woman's Sights on the Emigrant Trail.* Interview recorded by Matilda G. Bancroft. Salem, OR, 1878. BANC MSS P-A 17.

Cooke, Sarah A. *Theatrical and Social Affairs in Utah.* Interview by Matilda G. Bancroft. Salt Lake City, 1884. BANC MSS P-F 19 V. 1.

Coronel Collection. Film. [c. 1824–99.] BANC MSS C-B 940. The originals are in the Los Angeles County Museum.

Deady, Matthew P. Letters, dictations, and related biographical material, 1874–89. BANC MSS P-A 161.

Douglas, Sir James. Private papers, 1821–1861. BANC MSS P-C 12-13.

Evans, Elwood. *Northwest Coast History.* Olympia, WA, 1878. BANC MSS P-B 9.

Gomez, Vicente P. *Lo que sabe sobre cosas de California.* 1876. MSS C-D 90.

Hartnell, William Edward Petty. Papers, 1815–52. BANC MSS C-B 665.

Hayes, Benjamin. Papers, 1849–64. BANC MSS C-B 80-82.

Knight, William H., editor. *Hand-book Almanac for the Pacific States.* San Francisco, CA: H. H. Bancroft and Co.: 1862. XF851.H27.

Larkin, Thomas O. Papers, 1839–56. BANC MSS C-B 37-45.

Minto, John. *Early Days of Oregon.* Salem, OR, 1878. BANC MSS P-A 50.

Nidever, George. *Life and Adventures of George Nidever, A Pioneer of California since 1834.* Santa Barbara, CA, 1878. BANC MSS C-D 133.

Oak, Henry L. *Catalog of Books and Pamphlets in Bancroft Library.* Vol. 21, series 2. 1879. BANC MSS B-C 7.

Requena, Manuel. *Documentos para la historia de la California: Archivo de la Familia Requena.* 1877. BANC MSS C-B 92.

Richards, Franklin D. Letters and notes on Utah history, 1883–85. BANC MSS P-F 66 V. 1.

Ross, John. *Narrative of an Indian Fighter.* Manuscript. Jacksonville, OR, 1878–1895. BANC MSS P-A 63.

Savage, Thomas. *Documentos para la historia de la California.* 1874. BANC MSS C-B 48.

Sepúlveda, Ignacio. Letter to Hubert H. Bancroft, July 9, 1874, Los Angeles. BANC MSS C-E 65.

Strong, William. *History of Oregon.* Portland, OR, 1878. BANC MSS P-A 68.

Sutter, John A. *Personal Reminiscences of John A. Sutter.* 1876. BANC MSS C-D 14.

Swan, James G. *Washington Sketches.* Port Townsend, WA. BANC MSS P-B 20.

Taylor, Alexander Smith. Papers, 1864–72. BANC MSS C-B 663.

Vallejo, Mariano G. *Historia de la California.* BANC MSS C-D 17-21.

———. Letters to H. H. Bancroft. Records of the Library and the Publishing Companies. BANC MSS B-C 7.

Victor, Frances F. *All Over Oregon and Washington.* San Francisco: J. S. Carmany, 1872. F881.V63.

———. *Eleven Years in the Rocky Mountains and Life on the Frontier.* Hartford, CT: Columbian Book Company, 1877. F721 V5.

Warner, J. J. *Reminiscences of Early California.* 1873–77. BANC MSS C-D 23.

Wright, Doris M. *A Guide to the Mariano Guadalupe Vallejo Documentos para la Historia de California.* Guide. 1780–1875. BANC MSS C-B 1-36.

ABOUT THE EDITOR

K IM BANCROFT is a longtime teacher turned editor and writer. She earned a BA in English from Stanford, an MA in English and a teaching credential from San Francisco State University, and a PhD in education from UC Berkeley. She has taught at various high schools and community colleges in the Bay Area, at the Universidad de Guanajuato in Mexico, and at Sacramento State. Her classroom livelihood always included conversations about culture, society, and identity. Kim has edited several memoirs, including *Ariel: A Memoir* (Ariel Imago Publishing, 2012); *The Morning the Sun Went Down,* by Darryl Babe Wilson (Heyday, 1998); and *Ruth's Journey: A Survivor's Memoir* (University Press of Florida, 1996). She lives in a redwood forest in Willits, California, and enjoys the nouveau-Thoreau challenges and opportunities of life in a small cabin with a satellite dish on top.

INDEX

HEYDAY
into California

ABOUT HEYDAY

H EYDAY is an independent, nonprofit publisher and unique cultural institution. We promote widespread awareness and celebration of California's many cultures, landscapes, and boundary-breaking ideas. Through our well-crafted books, public events, and innovative outreach programs we are building a vibrant community of readers, writers, and thinkers.

THANK YOU

It takes the collective effort of many to create a thriving literary culture. We are thankful to all the thoughtful people we have the privilege to engage with. Cheers to our writers, artists, editors, storytellers, designers, printers, bookstores, critics, cultural organizations, readers, and book lovers everywhere!

We are especially grateful for the generous funding we've received for our publications and programs during the past year from foundations and hundreds of individual donors. Major supporters include:

Anonymous (4); Alliance for California Traditional Arts; Arkay Foundation; Judy Avery; James J. Baechle; Paul Bancroft III; BayTree Fund; S. D. Bechtel, Jr. Foundation; Barbara Jean and Fred Berensmeier; Berkeley Civic Arts Program and Civic Arts Commission; Joan Berman; John Briscoe; Lewis and Sheana Butler; California Civil Liberties Public Education Program; Cal Humanities; California Indian Heritage Center Foundation; California State Parks Foundation; Keith Campbell Foundation; Candelaria Fund; John and Nancy Cassidy Family Foundation, through Silicon Valley Community Foundation; Charles Edwin Chase; Graham Chisholm; The Christensen Fund; Jon Christensen; Community Futures Collective; Compton

GETTING INVOLVED

To learn more about our publications, events, membership club, and other ways you can participate, please visit www.heydaybooks.com.